THE ART OF

SMITHMARK

THE ART OF

QUEEN

THE eYe

ACKNOWLEDGMENTS

QUEEN are:
John Deacon, Brian May, Freddie Mercury, Roger Taylor

Management by Jim Beach

THE ART OF QUEEN THE EYE
Edited by Richard Ashdown and Tim Massey
Designed by Richard Gray
Written by David McCandless and Richard Ashdown
Lyrics reproduced by kind permission

With thanks to the following people who have all contributed to the making of
QUEEN THE EYE:
Mario Aguera, Marjit Bedi, Arnaud Bordet, David Bowry, Remi Brun, Amanda Cleverley,
Christophe Correani, Deano Crathern, Graham Crow, Paul Darrow, Vincent Desval,
Sally Gallagher, Cedric Gallet, Julie Glover, Richard 'Scotty' Graham, Martin Groves,
Odile Hadey, Dan Haley, Richard Harding, Ed Hayden, Francoise Jacob, Stuart Law,
Janet Lees Price, Loie Lefort, Bertrand Le Goff, Josh Macrae, Christophe Margon,
Anne Meyer, Colin Neilens, Martin Nicholas, William Nicolai, Clare Osborne,
Gary Parker, Jacqueline Pearce, Bay Rigby, Matt Risley, Damien Rochford, Tim Round,
Justin Shirley-Smith, Phil Symes, David Thierry, Matthew Tidbury, William Timms,
Peter Tuddenham, Vicky Vocat, Carl Wenczek.

Special thanks to:
Ken Berry, Shelagh Macleod, Martin Haxby, Jeremy Silver and all at EMI

Official Queen website: http://queen-fip.com
Official International Queen Fan Club:
The Old Bakehouse, 16a High Street, Barnes, London SW13 9LW

QUEEN THE EYE, THE ACTION GAME
Designed, developed and produced by Destination Design Limited
for Queen Multimedia Limited
Artwork and graphics by Rapid Eye Movement Limited E-Mail: rapid@rapideye.co.uk
Queen The Eye logo designed by Richard Gray
Distributed on PC CD-ROM by Electronic Arts Limited

This edition published in 1998 by SMITHMARK Publishers,
a division of U.S. Media Holdings, Inc.,
115 West 18th Street, New York, NY 10011.

SMITHMARK books are available for bulk purchase for sales promotion
and premium use. For details write or call the manager of special sales,
SMITHMARK Publishers, 115 West 18th Street, New York, NY 10011.

ISBN: 0 7651 9126 1

Printed in Singapore by Tien Wah Press

10 9 8 7 6 5 4 3 2 1

CONTENTS

JOHN DEACON

BRIAN MAY

FREDDIE MERCURY

ROGER TAYLOR

QUEEN

THIS BOOK HAS BEEN SPECIALLY COMPILED

TO CAPTURE THE LOOK AND FEEL OF OUR

FIRST ACTION ADVENTURE COMPUTER GAME

QUEEN THE EYE

AND TO EXPLAIN AND ILLUSTRATE

HOW THE IMAGES WERE CREATED.

QUEEN, LONDON, SEPTEMBER 1996.

The Plaza in the Works Domain.

We Must All See To Believe

The Credo Of The Eye

A revolution is gathering pace in the entertainment world. CD-ROM technology is bringing closer the dream of interactive movies. The dream of truly taking part in totally engrossing naturalistic worlds. Of immersing yourself in a tidal wave of sound and vision.

The flat, two dimensional sprites of yesterday are dying. In their place - photo-quality graphics and breath-takingly alive motion-captured models. While the realism of the images and dynamics of movement draw you in, the music and sound arouses your emotions.

Games are becoming an art form.

Queen are the first band to realise this. Using the latest technology, Queen and their developers, Destination Design, have modelled what will be the blueprint for other games to follow. Queen: The Eye - the first truly artistic game. It goes beyond any interactive music CD, beyond any cutting-edge console, beyond any classic game of the last five years.

The imagery of the game has been inspired by the musical iconography of Queen. Their music provides the soundtrack, a rich audio landscape for the action. The game bathes in the pathos of a classical story-line. It throws characters, plot twists, combat, drama, mystery, and expansive worlds at the player. It captivates, stimulates, and inspires, layered through out with the stunning music of Queen. It is a uniquely playable gaming experience. It intoxicates the eyes, the ears, and the mind. An arch fusion of the real and the computer generated. A rich concoction of imagery and music and entertainment, it is the first true melding of both the music industry and the video game market.

It is more interactive epic than game.

Is this the real life
Is this just fantasy
Caught in a landslide
No escape from reality
Open your eyes
Look up to the skies and see...

Bohemian Rhapsody

THE EYE

The not too distant future. Cyber technology has reached its apotheosis. The world has been devastated by global recession. Famine and poverty are rife. Democratic governments have crumbled. The status quo is shattered. In its place has risen a new world order. A malevolent oppressive regime, ruled by a bio-electronic despot. A self-replicating, cybernetic demi-god called The Eye.

THE NETWORK

What remains of urban society is dominated by The Network - a half-world where the physical and the computer-generated have become one. An extension of The Eye, it controls the population, suffocating, stifling, suppressing any creative thought or deed. Reality and illusion are blurred. Normal rules of life and death, freedom and spirit have ceased to exist.

THE CONTROLLERS

The Network is patrolled by The Controllers, ruthless agents of The Eye. Trained-killers, single-minded and deadly. They police the network, purging corrupting ideas and all forms of creativity and art. They seek out deviants and fugitives whose only crime is to express an individual thought or question the righteousness of the State. They bleach the network of this detritus. Keep it clean and pure.

MUSIC

Since the beginning of its reign, The Eye had been aware of a strange resonance. Powerful and rhythmic, it pulsed at the back of The Eye's mind, emanating from the Network's hidden archives. Even though the last vestiges of expression had been burnt from the eye-sockets of humanity, the resonance continued. Fear and a strange desire forced the Eye into action. It roved the areas, searching for the source of this macabre vibration. When it found the source, The Eye knew terror for the first time.

DEATH ON TWO LEGS

Too large to contain and too powerful to destroy, the music clamoured for escape, threatening to overcome the blackened heart of Network in a tidal wave of creativity and passion. In panic, the Eye sealed off the archives' alternate domains with impenetrable barriers and created a character, a guardian, to stalk and purge them. This entity was never given a name, but soon became known as Death On Two Legs.

DUBROC

On the other side of the barriers, the State ground on, unaware of the discovery. The Eye ruled supreme and its controllers did its bidding. The most powerful and faithful of The Controllers was Dubroc. He embodied the State's credo and carried out the will of The Eye with a terrifying fervour. Those who disobeyed were punished. Those who questioned were punished. He never disobeyed or questioned.

Then, by accident, Dubroc stumbled across a strange access port. He, too, had found the musical archive. He stood, stupefied, as a crescendo of sounds and images washed over him, paralysing him. Realisation dawned. The ideology of the State splintered before his eyes. He saw for the first time the cruelty of his world, the brutality of the regime, and the evil of The Eye.

PUNISHMENT

Before he could react, Death On Two Legs snaked out from the archives and clutched at his throat. Controllers appeared around him, overcoming him, wrestling him to the floor. He was dragged away, interrogated, beaten, and finally sentenced. He was a state traitor. He was a criminal. A fugitive. He had disobeyed and questioned the sanctity of the State.

Like those he had condemned before, Dubroc was sentenced to death...

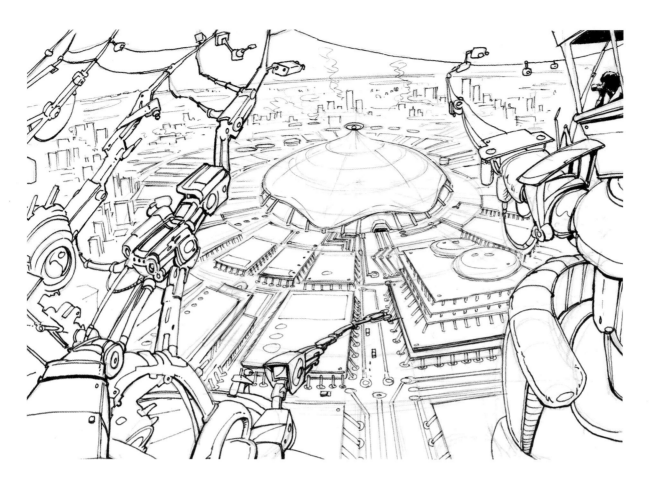

Original concept drawings of the apocalyptic future.

The Arena.

Street scene.

BEHIND THE SCENES: IN THE BEGINNING...

It's taken a twenty two man team thirty three man years to put together. It contains miles of rendered virtual landscapes, five CDs worth of data, and over a gigabyte of textures and still images. Six hundred camera angles frame over thirty characters and one hundred real-time objects. Nearly a thousand motion-captured moves and two hours of human voices bring the characters to life. Fifty five tracks total over 90 minutes of original music alongside thirty clips from fifteen Queen videos. The development of the ground-breaking Queen: The Eye has been an epic in itself.

Four years ago, two paths crossed. Tim Massey, a business man specialising in the licensing of film and entertainment properties, was introduced to Queen. The band were very interested by the potential of CD-ROM technology, the way it had blossomed beyond the bedroom into the music and film industries, and were looking for some way to bring their music into this arena.

The two parties agreed to work together, look into the area, but not rush into anything. The market was in flux, rising and falling as the nascent technology developed. At that time, CD-ROM's were just beginning to overtake cartridges as the de facto entertainment delivery medium of the nineties. Games were becoming a major currency. Top-selling titles could sell as well as the chart singles. The technology was coming of age. Digital audio on a game CD could now be played alongside the action, providing for the first time a unique way for musical artists to interact with their audience.

Queen wanted to find a product which did justice to their music, something which embodied the Queen ethos, bear-hugged the new technology, broke new ground, and satisfied the continents of fans who had followed the band for a quarter of a century. An obvious route beckoned. Something along the lines of the interactive anthology other bands had brought out - essentially album, video, and sleeve notes mixed into one. These titles had become the music industry's formula for embracing CD-ROM's. Queen however decided to skirt this path. They decided they wanted something different. They wanted an experience, something you could get involved and immersed in. Not a point'n'click Queen anthology, but rather something inspired by Queen, something which used their music and their imagery. They decided to produce a game.

The first step was to find the talent and the technology to create such an ambitious project. Very keen to invest in British talent and avoid relying on the current cradles of the gaming industry - the US and Japan - Queen trawled the massive gene-pool of UK talent. They found Richard Ashdown, a talented games producer and Stuart Law, a technical visionary who had both sharpened their experience in entertainment, technology and games with Electronic Arts. They shared Queens vision for a mould-breaking 'interactive epic' and together with Tim Massey they formed the nucleus of the production team.

The vision was that of a game, not tritely starring the members of Queen nor blandly tracking the history of the group through the decades, but rather a fully playable experience, a game naturally enhanced by the music and the art of Queen. Turning convention on its head, it wouldn't take the music and attach something to it - it would do it the other way round. The result: Queen: The Eye, a wholly artistic and creative endeavour, seamlessly blending story and plot and character with technology and music.

For this mammoth task, Destination Design Ltd. was formed, originally a production team, co-ordinating and guiding separate, subcontracted artists and programmers. However, it soon became clear that the scale and ambition of the project required more focus, more control. A decision was made to boost the company into a fully-fledged development house, to bring the Queen: The Eye project to fruition. Within four months, it had swelled from a four man production team to a fully operative development group consisting of software engineers, animator and support personnel - all housed under one roof in Windsor. Alongside this Destination Design Ltd. subcontracted the art work to artist group Rapid Eye Movement Ltd.

Together, this talented group of individuals worked for months, pain-stakingly designing, coding and piecing together the disparate elements which make up what you see before you today... The Art Of Queen: The Eye.

THE CINEMATIC INTRO

A cinematic intro at the beginning of Queen: The Eye springboards the player into the murky fog of Dubroc's grimy industrialised world.

Completely rendered in 3D, fully animated, and using the latest visual effects, the intro tells the story of Dubroc's discovery of the archives, his capture, his interrogation by Kazan, and his eventual sentencing to certain death in the Arena. The sequence is paced and directed like the beginning of an action adventure film, in short, sharp scenes. Sounds and music slowly crescendo. The lighting is dark and foreboding, Tyranny and impending conflict churn in the shadows. The rusty realism of the artwork highlights the stark, industrial look of the The Eye's oppressive world. The narrative quickly accelerates, reaching an abrupt climax, propelling the player into the fast paced immediacy of the Arena.

The intro is a stylish way of setting the scene. In a short space of time, we see the whole framework of the story - Dubroc change of attitude, the repressed archives, Death On Two Legs, The Eye's malevolence - and also our first glimpse of Kazan, the Eye's right-hand woman, whose determination and moral sense will plague - and maybe aid - Dubroc throughout the game.

THE GAME

The idea is simple. Dubroc must survive to find a way to defeat The Eye, free the musical archives and so free his world. After surviving the Arena, he must find his way through the four Queen Domains, the chaotic, overlapping collages, where reality and imagery collide. They are the flip-side of the oppressive order of The Eye. From the macabre renaissance environment of the Works Domain through the Theatre Domain - familiar yet not - to the disturbingly surreal Innuendo Domain and the mechanised peril of The Final Domain. The Domains both dazzle and disturb with their imagery.

In each of these parallel domains, Dubroc must find a key - the icons based on alchemy. These will be used later within the mechanism of the metal colossus - the Juggler - to restore the balance of the domains, and liberate the powers of music, creativity and freedom from the sealed archives. Then, Dubroc must take on and vanquish The Eye itself.

But, as Dubroc will find, these are bitter sweet worlds. The Watchers he must defeat in the Arena are nothing compared to the perils and dangers which lie beyond. Hidden secrets, mysterious characters, cerebral puzzles, deadly scenery - all will test his agility and intelligence to the limit.

Beyond that still is the relationship between Dubroc and his Superior, the female controller Kazan. She is the one who discovers Dubroc accessing the archives and it is her again who will become mistress of his fate within the domains, as she is sent by The Eye to pursue him. Whether she becomes his nemesis or ally will depend upon the skill of the player. To compound things, Dubroc is also stalked throughout by the horrific creature 'Death on Two Legs' - the avatar of The Eye. In its many deadly forms, it destroys and murders everything in its path. And now, it has Dubroc's scent.

The spike collapses puncturing the membrane of the Arena.

THE CHARACTERS

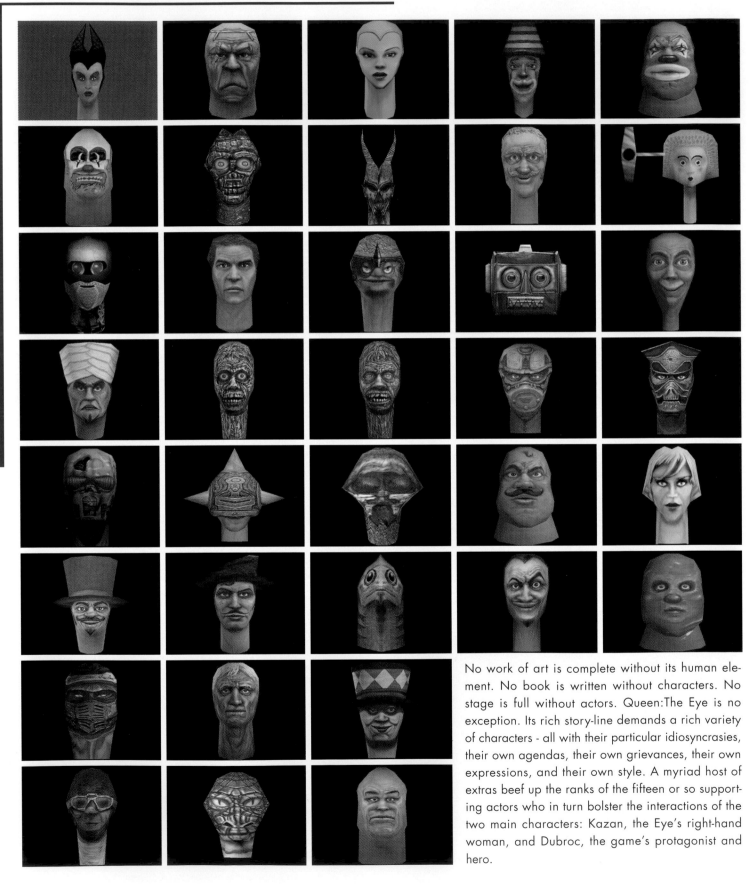

No work of art is complete without its human element. No book is written without characters. No stage is full without actors. Queen:The Eye is no exception. Its rich story-line demands a rich variety of characters - all with their particular idiosyncrasies, their own agendas, their own grievances, their own expressions, and their own style. A myriad host of extras beef up the ranks of the fifteen or so supporting actors who in turn bolster the interactions of the two main characters: Kazan, the Eye's right-hand woman, and Dubroc, the game's protagonist and hero.

DUBROC

Synchronise your minds and see the beast within him rise

Flick Of The Wrist

Dubroc is the central character in the Queen: The Eye. A rakish anti-hero who once strutted, powerful and authoritative, through the Network. Now, thrown into the Queen Domains, Dubroc is a man out of time. Rootless and displaced, betrayed and cast-out, he is a pariah with a bleak future. His belief-systems lie in tatters around his feet. The foundations of his life have turned out to be false. The Eye, once his God, is now his enemy. The controllers, his fellow bleachers, will now eradicate him. Beyond the Arena - if he ever escapes - Dubroc will find himself in an alien universe, dwarfed by symbols, engulfed by music and light and passion.

Making the protagonist of a computer game interesting, unusual, and believable is not easy. Little more than a bundle of polygons, Dubroc's presence on screen and the sympathy he draws from the audience is dependant on the careful manicuring of his image, and the microscopic attention to detail paid to every word he says 'in character'. His fighting ability and massive range of combat moves obviously work to endear him to the more gung-ho player, but he needs to be endowed with depth, sensitivity, and a certain wholeness of personality to satisfy those more interested in the rich strain of adventure and mystery in the game.

DUBROCK

Once I could see
the good in me
The black and the white
distinctively colouring
Holding the world inside
Now all the world
is grey to me...

The Night Comes Down

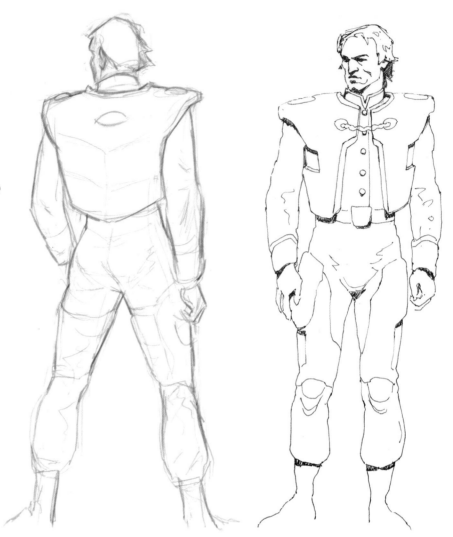

Originally, Dubroc was going to be a young character - gangly, enthusiastic but lethal. However, the character matured as the game developed, from youthful vigour to hardened professional. In turn his face became more furrowed, more etched with time. Finally, his age settled at a toughened, hardened, athletic thirty-something.

CHARACTER

Dubroc is an interesting character. He is hero and anti-hero rolled into one - the archetypal Dystopian hero. Dark and light. His previous life and hideous reputations as a brutal controller haunt him. Yet the sights and sounds of these new parallel worlds lead him in, and inspire him to achieve the only atonement possible - destroying The Eye.

When you're dealing with this level of realism in graphics you have to deal with expression.

The soul in torment is reflected in the way he has been drawn. His face has a pinched, world-weary expression, resigned yet alert, unhappy yet determined. He is set on surviving and having his vengeance on the Eye. This is also conveyed by the way he moves. His gait, his combat moves, even the way he turns his head have been played with emotion by the actor during motion capture, and then exaggerated in post-production by the 3D artists. He has a cat-like furtiveness about him, coupled with the laid back nonchalance of a hardened fighter.

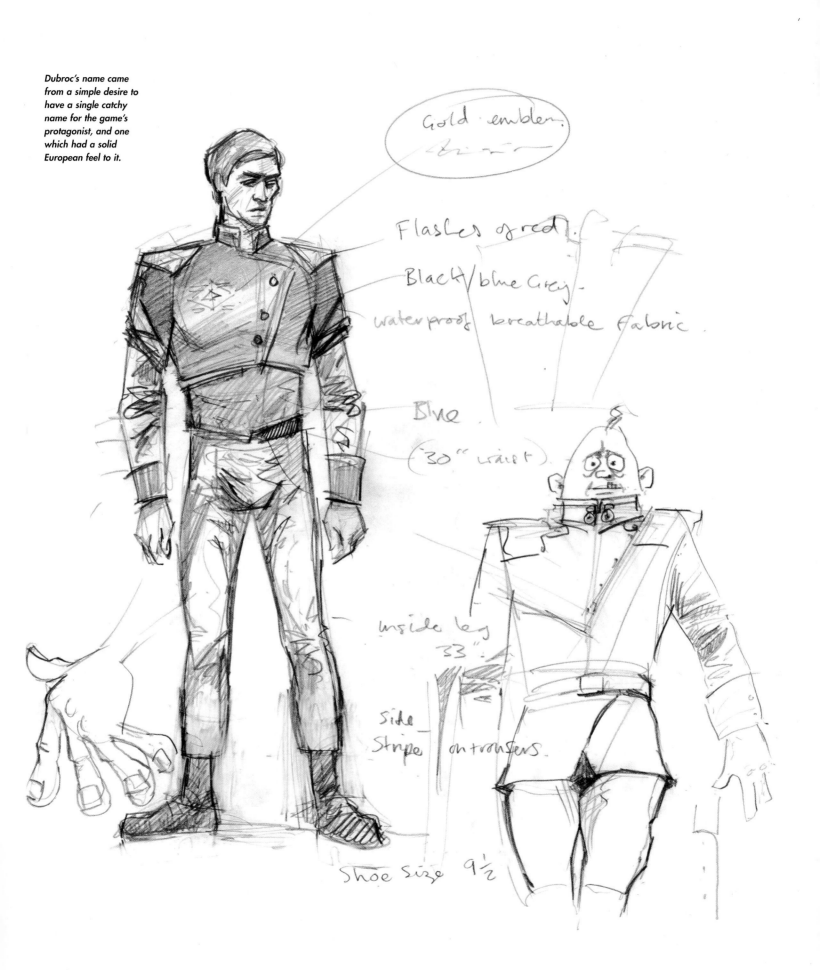

Dubroc's name came from a simple desire to have a single catchy name for the game's protagonist, and one which had a solid European feel to it.

Gold emblem.

Flashes of red.

Black/blue Grey.

waterproof breathable fabric

Blue

("30" waist)

inside leg
33"

side
stripe on trousers.

Shoe size 9½

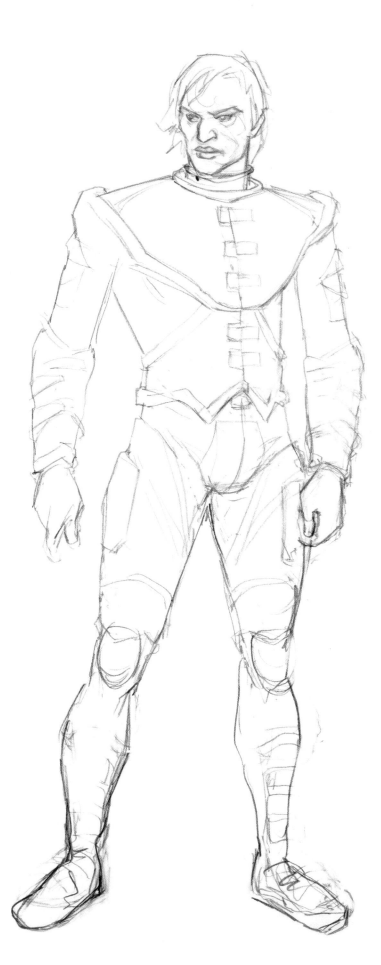

HERO

Dubroc was at the centre of the original creative ideas - a strong composite of various adventure heroes and Sci-fi characters from popular culture. Initially, Indiana Jones was the strongest influence, his swashbuckling and unbelievable resourcefulness as good a backbone for any hero. But then, the character took a dark, more rogue-ish turn, heading for something more like Avon in Blake's Seven, the classical amoral character with a heart.

As the game and story-line developed, the theme of Queen music running through the game began to demand a certain spirituality from Dubroc - a side of him which could only be awoken by exposure to the Archives. Avon soon fell by the way side. Momentarily, Dubroc became a French Algerian character and then, eventually and finally, a futuristic Navaho Indian type hero. The native Indian look and feel to the character perfectly matched the need for a spiritual action protagonist, who could swiftly switch from solving the age-old riddles of alchemy to defeating servants of The Eye.

MORALITY

Central to Dubroc's character and indeed to any classic protagonist in literature is morality. The ethical framework of a person is often the first thing the reader, or in this case, the player shares. While writing the script for Queen: The Eye, Richard Ashdown was painfully aware of this, and the necessity to implement a morality choice for the Dubroc character as early as possible within the game.

Particular instances occur during game, exposing Dubroc to 'morale choices'. Some, like attempting to help The Professor's assistant in The Arena, are 'do or die' situations. If the player ignores what's going on around him, he pays the price - death in this case, since the assistant has vital last minute information about the Arena.

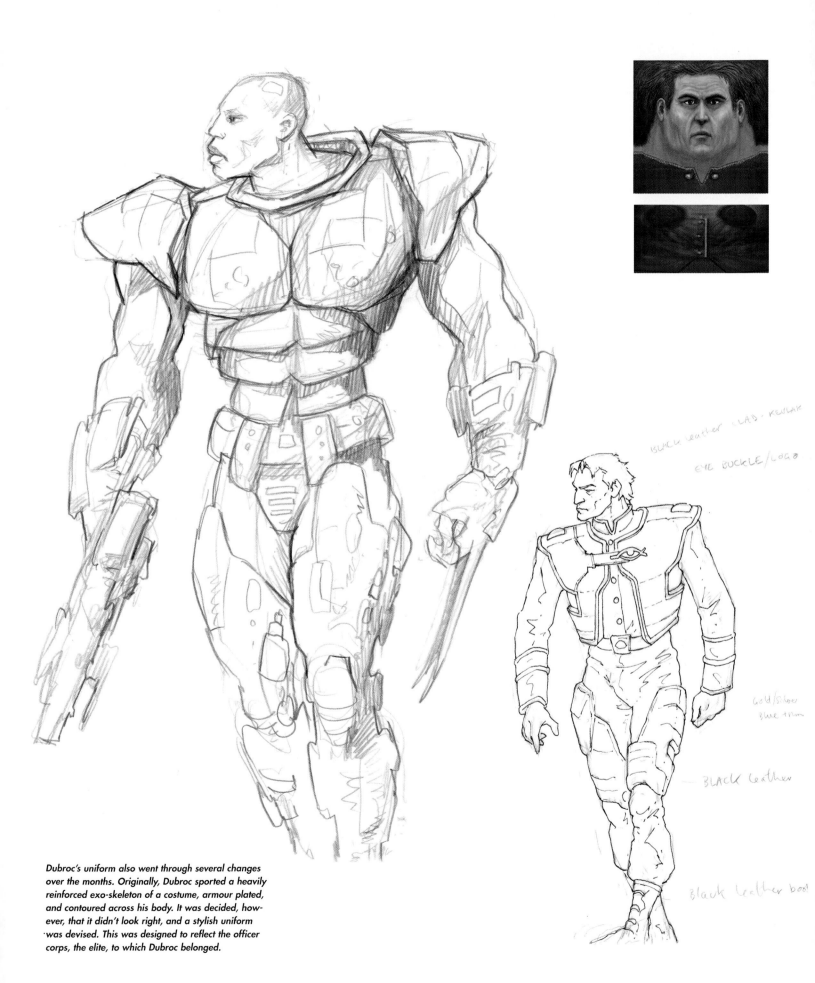

Black leather clad - kevlar

Eye buckle/logo

Gold/silver
Blue trim

BLACK leather

Black leather boot

Dubroc's uniform also went through several changes over the months. Originally, Dubroc sported a heavily reinforced exo-skeleton of a costume, armour plated, and contoured across his body. It was decided, however, that it didn't look right, and a stylish uniform was devised. This was designed to reflect the officer corps, the elite, to which Dubroc belonged.

KAZAN

Of course, no central character is complete without an alter-ego, a partner-in-crime, or sidekick. Dubroc is no exception, and his comes in the nubile form of Kazan, fellow controller, and simultaneous aid and obstacle on Dubroc's quest.

She's half-way between a manga heroine and a female Doc Holiday in High Noon. When she's in a scene, it's not clear whether she's going to help or not. The game is dependent as much on the player's actions as it is on Kazan's agenda. This introduces an unpredictable human element to the game.

Games of this genre have game-play designed to drive the player towards certain goals, which in turn lead them to other targets, and so on down the flowchart. Kazan pushes the player down certain paths or helps when the puzzles seem insoluble.

Like Dubroc, Kazan's appearance has been refined over the entire course of the game's development. Originally, being The Eye's right-hand woman, she had a vaguely bio-technological look, decked in a chrome cyborg outfit, with blood red hair, and a huge tattoo curling round her body - more of an assassin than a character. She soon developed however, loosing the more dominatrix look for a more down-to-earth appearance, with a blonde cropped functional haircut, large unclassically good looking features, and the same brand of Controller uniform as Dubroc.

"We're in a parallel universe Dubroc - or did you miss out Chaos Theory at school ? Listen, whatever we do here is going to have an impact on our own domains. We might destroy our own world by our actions here. So take care. I want to get back in one piece."

Kazan, dialogue from the game.

KAZAN
in Armour

She is, of course, like all modern screen heroines, good looking, tough, and able to give as good as she gets - physically and verbally. As a controller, she shares Dubroc's lithe athleticism and combat skills. She refuses to put up with any stupidity or lack of thought from anyone. When, in the Innuendo Domain, she comes into her own, she has a constant tirade of abuse ready for the often hapless player: "Are you mad? What can I do with an anvil?" she spits. "Dubroc - get real! Either show me something useful or leave me alone." At the same time she's not omniscient - and doesn't pretend to be. "Hmmm. Strange. I've no idea," she says, when Dubroc brandishes an obscure object at her.

Gradually, over the course of the game, the relationship between the two develops. At first Dubroc's enemy, Kazan soon mellows as the power of the Queen Domains begin to affect her. Her attitude to Dubroc's crime softens and she actually comes to like him ("As hard as it is for me to admit this, you're alright Dubroc"), trading insults and pushing the plot forward with her own inquisitiveness, until she is directly working with him to complete the game.

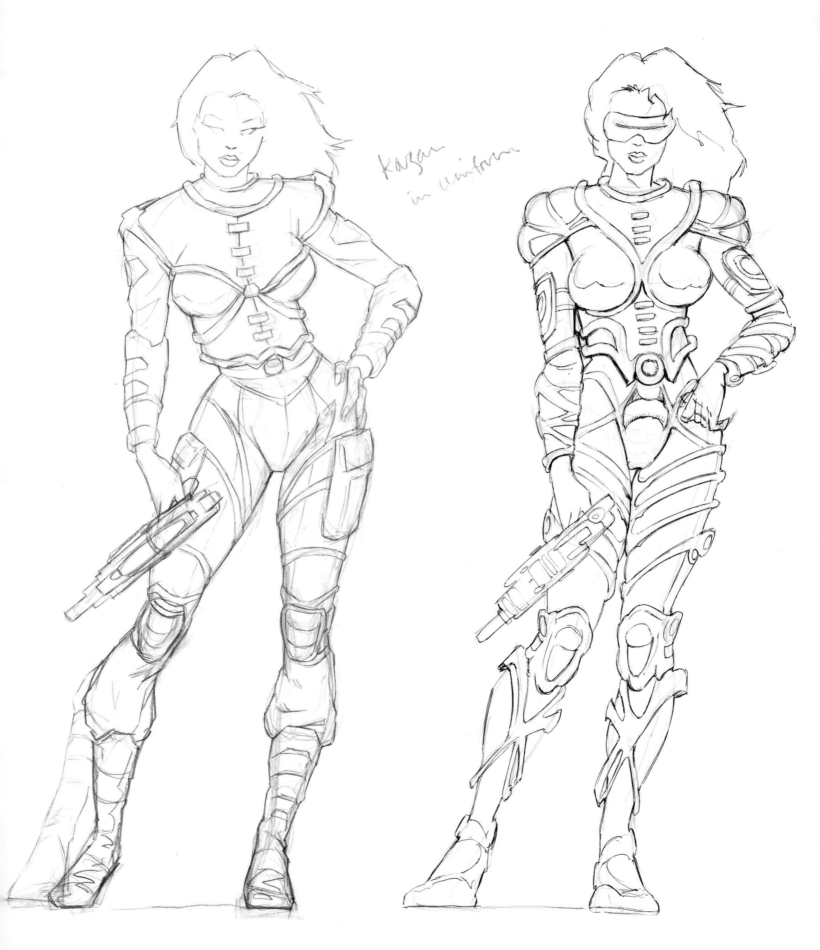

Kazan
in uniform

Storm the master marathon I'll fly through

By flash and thunder fire and I'll survive,

I'll survive, I'll survive

Then I'll defy the laws of nature

And come out alive

Then I'll get you...

Seven Seas of Rhye

KAZAN

THE ARENA

*Music is playing
in the darkness
And a lantern
goes swinging by
Shadows flickering
my heart's jittering...*

You And I

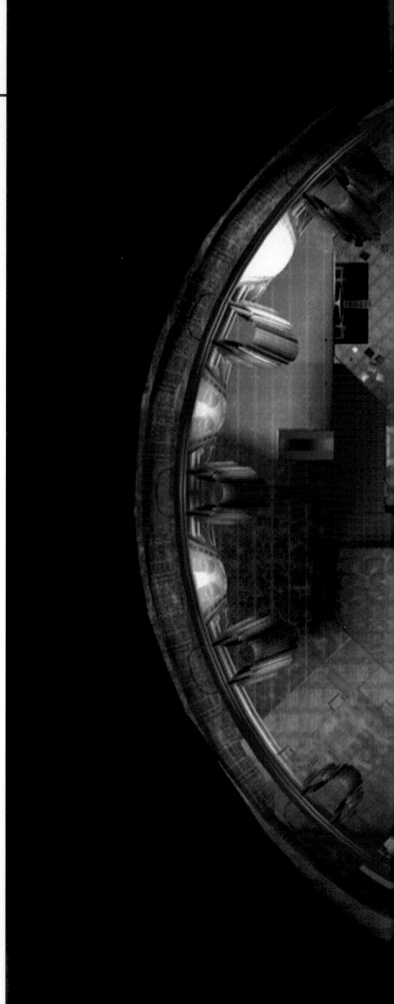

Many years ago, The Eye realised the need to entertain its people. It created the Arena, a huge domed edifice, a cruel maze where brutal gladiatorial combat and deadly traps serve to dispatch those criminals who have betrayed the State.

Over the years, the once ironically palatial architecture has folded in on itself. It has become rotted and warped. New deadlier elements have been grafted onto its surface. Limescale, sewage, and the blood and sweat of countless combatants have condensed over the scenery, rusting and corroding its splendour. Violence pockmarks the floors. Death stains the walls. The lights have failed. Makeshift bulbs create vast pockets of shadow, torches make vain clutches at the darkness. Neon flickers. The smell of dirt, and disease, and death is rank, suffocating.

Suspended above it all this decay is the central spike, a huge decaying representation of the Sword Of Damocles. Massive in size, the stone monolith dangles from the roof, taunting and luring luckless competitors with the promise of escape. The top of the spike is the only exit from The Arena. Few have reached this point. Fewer still have escaped.

INTO THE ARENA

Both a hunting ground and a prison, The Arena has been designed to 'absorb' those who criticise or attack the state. Even those hapless individuals who make the mistake of expressive individual thoughts or motives soon find themselves fighting to the death against the six Watchers - the gladiatorial champions - and the countless deranged security guards which patrol its labyrinthine intestines.

Most disturbingly, the Arena is also the only form of entertain permitted in the totalitarian regime of The Eye. For the drone population it supplies an exciting alternative to State-controlled television and propaganda broadcasts. They can jack into the Arena at local neon-emporiums and watch the action through the one-hundred or so strategically placed cameras. They can also place bets on which Watcher will deal the killing blow against the toughest challenger. In this case - Dubroc.

In the game, using a combination of agility, cartography, and sheer violence, Dubroc must circumvent the multiple perils of the Arena and find the way out. The Arena itself is shaped like a huge labyrinth, with a series of interconnecting levels - basement, ground floor, catwalks, and roof tops. Each one must be negotiated in turn to reach the giant spike, but blind corners, crumbling concrete, booby-trapped parapets, and the continuous presence of The Watchers make things less than easy.

There is a specific path and a specific set, but to actually reach the exit, Dubroc must have in his possession six crystal lodestones, used to activate the dais below the spike. Naturally, these keys are scattered around the extremities of the Arena, and heavily guarded by dangerous puzzles, state guards, and the ever present Watchers.

Each Watcher is released into the Arena via one of the gaping maws dotted around the periphery of the Arena. These entrances are protected by state troopers. The darkness beyond is often mistaken for an escape route by Arena competitors. Those who risk it have never returned to tell the tale.

Initially, Dubroc finds himself in one corner of the Arena. The sense of space is immense and Dubroc is dwarfed by the curved spinal walls and the seemingly organic dome. Far away in the distance, a rusted metal aerial catwalk drifts above a sea of effluent. Towering above is the massive central spike. Huge spikes jut from the floor and passages and tunnels burrow in all directions. Dotted around the sides at regular intervals are huge gaping maws - Watcher pods where the champions of the Arena emerge.

The Arena has an air of possession about it, as if some ancient civilisation had grown or built its organic, cathedral like interior, and it has since been colonised with humanity's relentless concrete and steel.

The Arena is alive with ambient noise. The scratching and grinding of unseen gears. The gurgling of sewage outlets. The mumbling and mindless chatter of the guards. The clanging of steel doors. The screams of dying competitors. A gunshot here. An explosion there. And behind it all, the scuttling and clawing and pattering of cockroaches, rats, beetles, and bats, scrabbling in the darkness.

The warehouse looks down into the disturbing interior of the pillar room. Some of the boxes here can be cracked open to find weapons, or pushed around and lifted to provide access to hidden areas. The wet floor glistens.

Down below the Warehouse, the distressed roof is supported by bizarrely ornate pillars. Thick and ribbed like cross between classical Egyptian columns and the geometry of the Incas. A bluish heat haze stifles the air in the room. The pock-marked floor is scummed with algae and jaundiced with age. Stalactites clog the windows. Rust runs down the walls. The scene is set for a deadly confrontation.

The Arena is dividing into areas of light, and dark, and half-lights, creating a dramatically deadly feel to the scenery. Old fashioned Allen gas lamps light most of the connecting corridors and hallways, casting weak pools of illumination, leaving huge swathes of architecture in darkness. Elsewhere, broad fluorescent bulbs create combat arenas from pools of light, while evocative footlight highlight the distorted dimensions of the scaffold maze area and the pillar room.

Aerial view of the
pillar room.

The pillar room.

39

The Mine Dispenser forms an unnerving landmark in the Arena. As Dubroc picks his way through the maze, he catches the odd glimpse of it in the distance. Eventually he finds it, and discovers that it provides access to the aerial catwalks which lead to the final dais. Unfortunately, too late, he realises it's booby-trapped. Mines are ejected from its core, scattering across the floor, and effectively blocking his only route back. He has no choice but to risk the nightmarish catwalk maze.

The prison room.

The store room.

The granite dais where the six keys must be used to release the magnetic locks.

The maze.

The aerial walkway is one of the last challenges Dubroc must face. Suspended far above the ground level of the Arena, the catwalks hang precariously from thin wires attached to the roof. Here and there, acid and corrosion have rotted away entire sections of the grated floor, leaving abyssian gaps for Dubroc to leap. Whirling blades and flame towers are scattered all around, forcing Dubroc to perform duck, jump, and roll combos at every turn.

The Arena is rife with architectural touches which will either help or hinder Dubroc. Alas the deadly architecture out-numbers the helpful. The whole Arena is one huge death-trap, a pressure-valve of peril. Each section is fraught with hidden danger. Flamers, for example, cover tar-pits and fulminate when Dubroc clambers over them, while pressure-mines rise from the floor at inopportune moments and explode. Spikes will do the same. Flame towers are more obviously placed but unpredictably spurt fire at erratic intervals.

Blades are also unpredictable. They either spring from the walls unexpectedly, cleanly disembowelling or decapitating competitors, or are in blatant display around the aerial catwalk, forcing extreme acrobatics for anyone navigating the section. Often working in tandem with the blades are blow darts, which spit from inconspicuous looking grooves in the walls. The deadly poison laden arrows cripple on contact.

The thin walkways and unguarded edges have to be carefully navigated as they are often trigger points for crumbling walkways. A false step could lead to fatal fall into the toxic effluent spill which churns its way through certain parts of the Arena.

The rusted cages of the aerial maze form a treacherous puzzle for Dubroc. The rotted steel walls do not provide much support and are prone to collapse. And the distinctive up-lighting creates a myriad of contradicting shadows off the walls and floors, confusing and disorientating.

The teleporter.

The central spike dangles oppressive from the darkened peak of the Arena's dome. At the top of the spike is a combat ring, encased in thin barriers where Dubroc must face the final Watcher and in victory, win his freedom.

The lava pit.

ARENA: GROUND LEVEL.

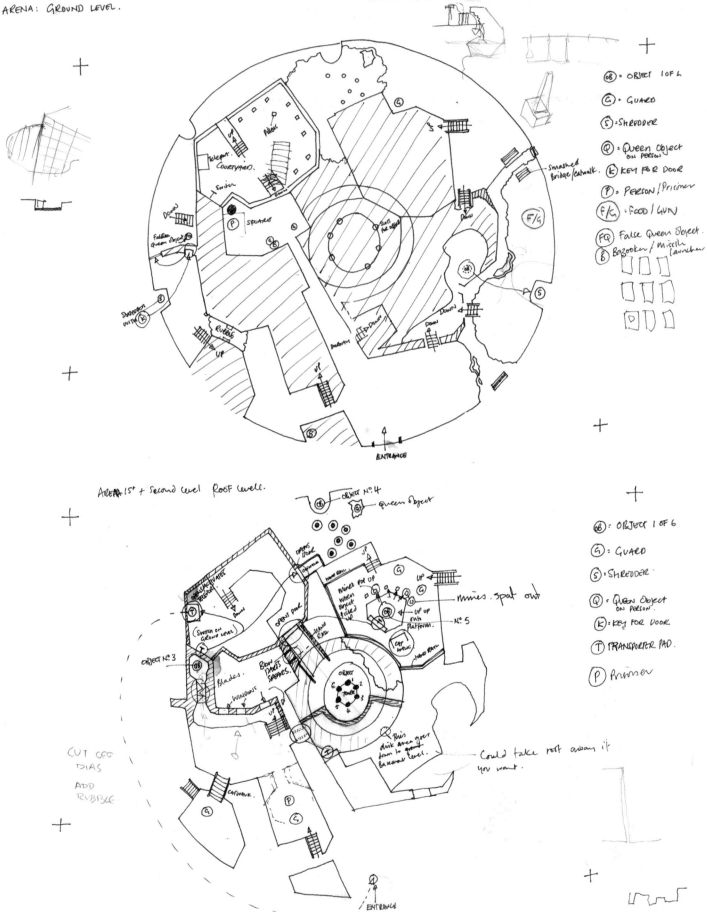

OB = OBJECT 1 OF 6
G = GUARD
S = SHREDDER
Q = QUEEN OBJECT ON PERSON
K = KEY FOR DOOR
P = PERSON / Prisoner
F/G = FOOD / GUN
FQ = False Queen Object.
B = Bazooka / Missile launcher

Smashed Bridge / catwalk

WEAPON COURTYARD.
Switch
SQUARE
Fallen Queen Object
Shredder WITH K
RUBBLE
UP
DOWN
Slots for mines
Down
Down
Down
UP
UP
ENTRANCE

AREAA 1st + second level   ROOF level.

OB = OBJECT 1 OF 6
G = GUARD
S = SHREDDER
Q = QUEEN OBJECT ON PERSON
K = KEY FOR DOOR
T = TRANSPORTER PAD.
P = Prisoner

OBJECT N° 4
Queen object
OBJECT N° 3
Object N° 3
(Switch on ground level)
Reactivate Reactor
Blades.
WINDOWS
OPEN POOL
OPENS DOOR
Blow Darts Spears.
Mines for UP when Person kicks
UP
mines. spat out
UP + over onto Platform.
N° 5
CAT WALK
HAND RAIL
HAND RAIL
OBJECT TOWER
This dark area goes down to ground. Backward level.
Could take roof away if you want.
CUT OFF DIAS
ADD RUBBLE
CATWALK.
G
P
S
ENTRANCE

46

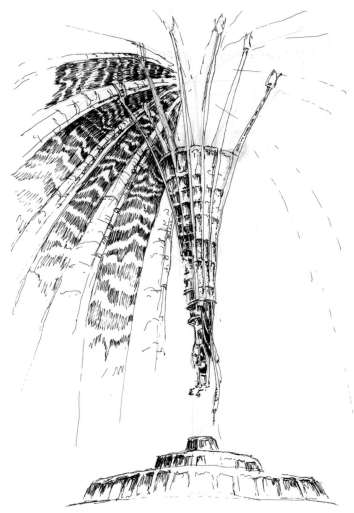

Original sketch of the spike.

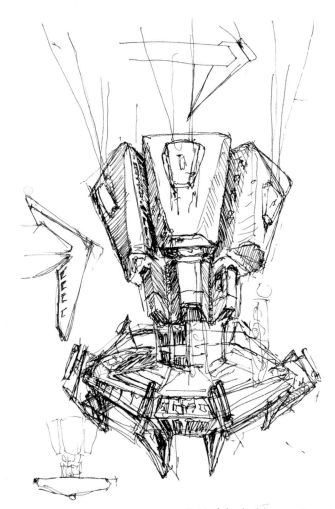

Original sketch of the mine dispenser.

From the earliest day of Queen: The Eye, the Arena was going to be circular, but originally, the design was going to be a more outlandish and actually based on an eyeball, with blood vessels, retinal patterns, and pupil metaphors coating the 3D shapes. A prototype was developed, populated with weird and wonderful textures, but eventually it was dropped for the more functional, yet still stylish 'blasted city' look.

The overall design started out on a piece of paper as a variety of circles, defining the areas within the Arena - the entrance, location one, location two and so on. Each of the four levels of the Arena was sketched out on a separate sheet of paper and then overlaid.

Over a few weeks, the design gradually became more complicated as detailed sections were developed, and architectural motifs decided on. The environment had to work from any angle.

Finally, after working with no spatial restrictions, the walls were added. Then the 3D artists and modellers went to work gluing the separate elements into a realistic and minutely detailed model.

Due to its circular nature and open-plan design, The Arena had to be worked as a single huge 3D model, thirteen megabytes in size with over 64,000 individual faces and five megabytes of textures. In real world terms, the dome was 100 metres in diameter, and each camera view took an hour to render at full quality.

fish head.
(Dragon)

Angel's looks are deceiving. Her green skin and blue skull cap give her an almost pixie-esque look, while her voluptuous figure distracts from the rows of serrated spikes jutting from her catsuit. Her wrists contain specialised circular saws which she whips out at the start of combat. Dubroc must be wary of her reverse slash attacks and her deadly groin-to-head upward slash special move. She is easily one of the most fastest and most lethal Watchers.

THE WATCHERS

Dubroc's main opponents in the Arena are the Watchers. These self-styled champions of the Arena are gladiatorial masters, ex-convicts and cybernetic experiments gone wrong. The Eye's failed attempt at genetic sculpture has left the six Watchers physically deformed and hideously psychotic, single-minded in their determination to seek out and kill competitors, relentlessly and without mercy. Some have physical enhancements. Some sport strange unexpected weaponry. Some are bio-mechanical. Some cannot be harmed by certain weapons. Each one has their own strength and weakness which Dubroc must isolate to avoid or exploit. Only his skill, speed and combat prowess can protect him against a Watcher.

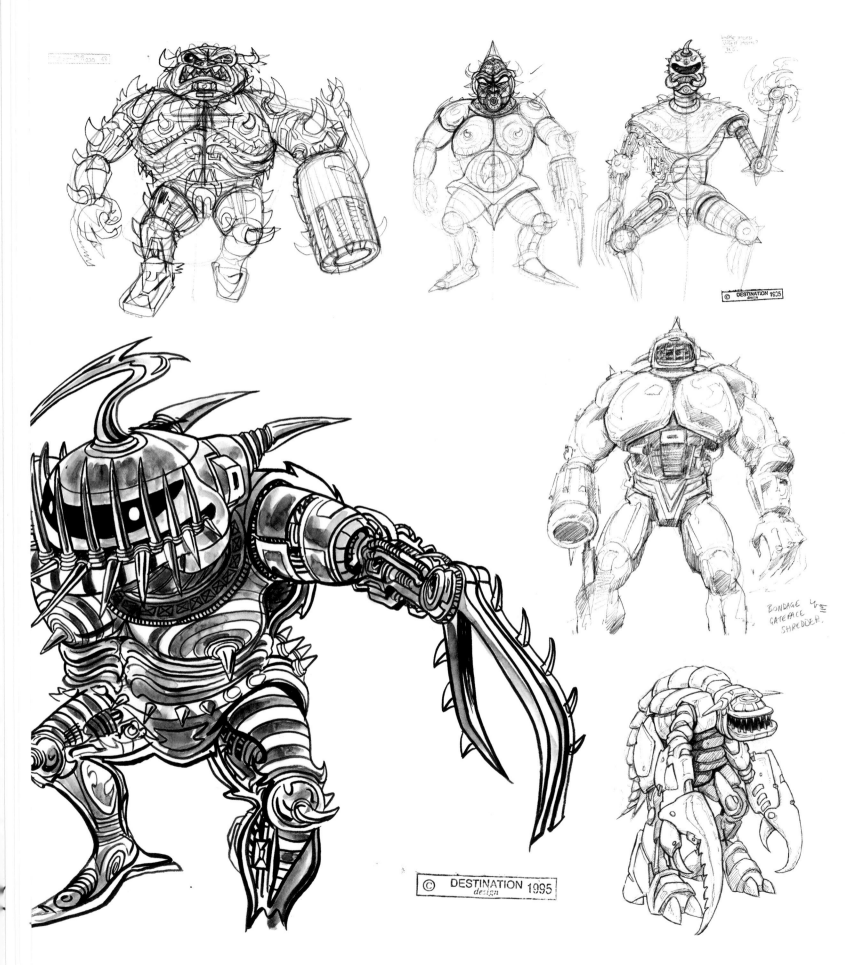

BONDAGE 4/5
GATEFACE
SHREDDER.

© DESTINATION design 1995

© DESTINATION design 1995

49

THE WORKS DOMAIN

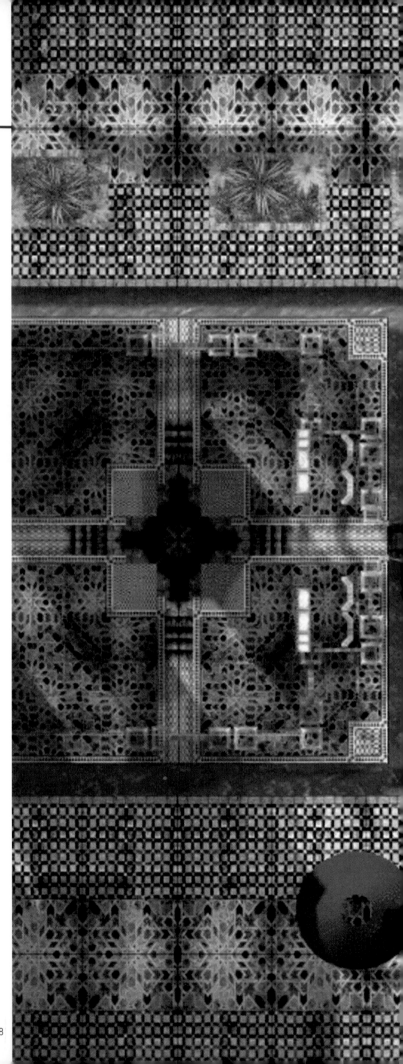

After crashing through the floor of The Arena, Dubroc drifts in unconsciousness. Purple and black colours flit across his mind. In the darkness, a sound enters his brain. Loud and undulating it drags him back into awareness.

He wakes to the mottled sunlight of the Works Domain. An Islamic prayer call fills his head. Around him rear architectural behemoths, huge stone buildings floating on a sea of polluted water, crumbling and derelict, encased in a sprawl of mist. Bridges lead from each edifice to the plaza, centred by a large alchemic Astrolabe. The whole scene is dominated by an awe-inspiring radio-tower which soars high above the rooftop, puncturing the shroud of fog. The air is damp and cloying. The prayer call drifts away, leaving a macabre, motionless quiet. Dubroc has discovered the Works Domain, an esoteric alternate place where the renaissance has gone badly wrong, and time has slowed to a gloomy crawl.

Here, architecture has gone mad. Masonry clogs the street. The buildings fold over themselves, cramped and huddled, a bizarre clash of renaissance Italy and post-modernist Barcelona. The Domain's landmarks encircle the plaza. To the west is the Museum and Library - once great halls of learning, now dead and clogged with dust. To the north, lies the expansive Ballroom, and to the east the once magnificent, now decrepit Crystal Palace. The rest of the buildings in the domain are mere shadows in the fog, bare shells, boarded up, dead.

Unwittingly, Dubroc has found himself in a war zone. The evil Baroness, Astaroth, and the benign Professor Cagliari are wrestling for control of the Works Domain. The Professor is the last obstacle for the Baroness' complete subjugation of the world, and she, with her thuggish army and swashbuckling Lover Prince, have occupied the Plaza and laid siege to the Professor's fortified tower. Now Dubroc will find himself drawn into this conflict as he searches, bewildered, for clues to his plight and a way out back to his own domain.

THE MUSEUM

The Museum forms a huge, oppressive presence in the Works Domain. Modelled in the heavy, leaning style of classic Romanesque buildings, this multi-tiered construction resembles a Renaissance mausoleum, its broad, squat facade stained with the smoke and the smog of time. The once grand building is protected by a carved stone gargoyle and a weighty stone bell. Rubble and fallen masonry blight its exterior. More gargoyles and demonic faces stand guard on its every corner. Massive cornices and architraves bolster its contours. Gloomy leaded glass windows frown out over the plaza. Huge rounded arches at its base support the massive weight of the super-structure. A clump of lesser buildings huddle around its rear and disappear anonymously into the mist. The Museum casts a sombre air over the entire Domain.

The entrance to the Museum is under the arches, through an ornate carved entrance portal. Unfortunately, a gargoyle mouth protects the door, greeting Dubroc with the riddle: "To proceed without danger you must strike the right tone. Only those beyond vanity can enter."

The Astrolabe in the Plaza.

The sumptuous interior of the Museum belies its oppressive facade. The main room, wide and expansive like the Natural History Museum in London, contains surreal exhibits. Dinosaur eggs in glass display cases. A stuffed figure of Icarus, dangling from the ceiling. A huge clock is at one end of the room. Mannequins of toys stand frozen here and there. An antique film projector machine sits quietly inactive. The walls are carved with arcane sigils. The room has an air of dangerous beauty. Dali-esque and deadly, the toy exhibits will come alive and attack Dubroc if the correct route isn't discovered.

Early sketches of the Clockwork monsters: a hideous doll, a broken articulated mannequin, and a deranged metal soldier.

The entrance to the Islamic inspired library.

The library has an undeniable Islamic feel to its design, like one of the great Andalusian libraries or a Moorish mosque. The high metal roof is corrugated and concave, inlaid with ornate ironwork, and draped with elaborate lamps which smoulder with incense. Kufic and naskh script is interwoven in gold on the walls, circling the curved windows, and running down the stylised ogee arches. Strange geometric shapes decorate the gaps. The whole room bathes in golden light. Peaceful quiet reigns. It has a solemn, religious, almost Masonic ambience.

The walls are covered with bookcases, on two levels. The ground level surrounds an area reserved for reading. The floor bears a strange quartered and colour-coded insignia - like a garish chess board.

Early sketch of The Lover Prince.

THE PRISON CELL AND SEWERS

Throughout his numerous battles and encounters in the Works Domain, Dubroc runs the risk of being defeated and captured. Sooner or later, he will loose a battle and, after being clubbed by his victorious assailant, awakens in the prison cell.

In keeping with the Domain's renaissance air, the local gaol is sepulchral and nasty. Built from huge timbers, jammed precariously together with rusted iron joints, the cells are dangerously decrepit. Poor exterior lighting casts dagger-like shadows across the walls. The stones slabs on the floor are matted with algae and limescale. The stench from the nearby sewers mingles with the dried sweat and blood of past prisoners. The bars are made from heavily rusted metal and flecked with some unspeakably viscous liquid.

Dark and dank, the sewer's murky depths contain repulsive effluent. Rotten timbers jut from the churning green sludge, propping up the cracked ceiling. Green lamps at regular intervals along the walls barely illuminate the thin walkways and arches which resemble a disused, distorted underground metro system. Monsters lurk in the darkness here, waiting for Dubroc to pass into range.

At the end of the sewers, Dubroc discovers a mysterious riddle, etched into the wall.

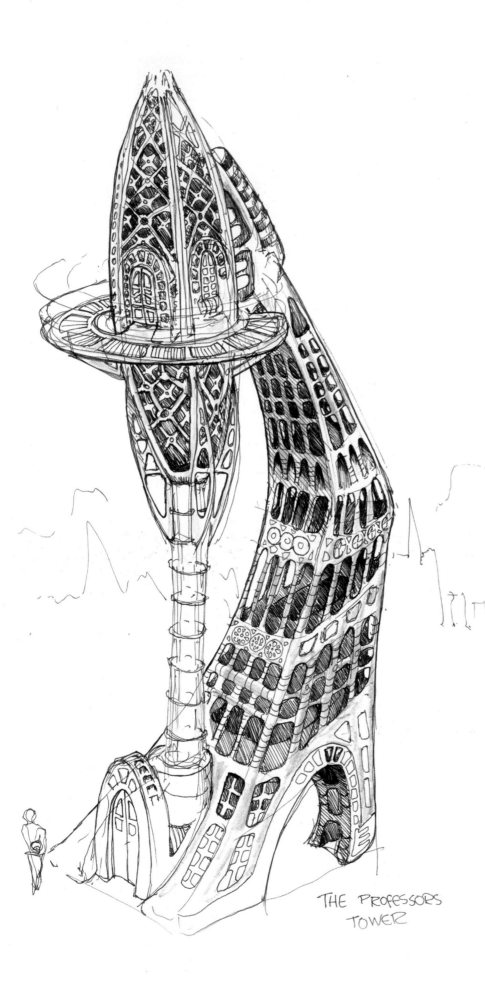

THE PROFESSORS
TOWER

THE PROFESSOR'S TOWER

By far the most dominating and distinctive landmark in the Works Domain is the Professor's Tower - an esoteric architectural concoction, combining the Sagrada Familia in Barcelona with a baroque rocket launching facility. Apparently the brainchild of the professor, the tower erupts from its foot-like base, curving spinally to form a huge gantry for the Professor's jewel-encrusted Victorian-style escape rocket. At the peak of the tower juts the radio mast, beaming its subversive signals across the entire Domain, sporadically dissipating the threatening silence which surrounds it. The tower is an incredibly ostentatious colossus, defying logic in its every turn and bejeweled corner, barely containing the massive intellect and ego within.

THE BALLROOM

To the north of the Plaza lies the Ballroom. Deep inside resides the Baroness and Aligheri her Lover Prince. The reigning royals of this Domain, they have constructed their palatial ballroom with an opulence rivalling Louis XIV. The airy hallways are brilliant with stained glass light. The central marble floor is dominated by a Rococo dome and the soaring elegance of a jewelled chandelier. Side rooms lead off to the rear, while a set of stairs lead expectantly to the Baroness's Boudoir.

Despite its bitter-sweet beauty, the Ballroom is a deadly location in the Works Domain, heavily patrolled by thuggish guards and the vengeful Lover Prince, Aligheri.

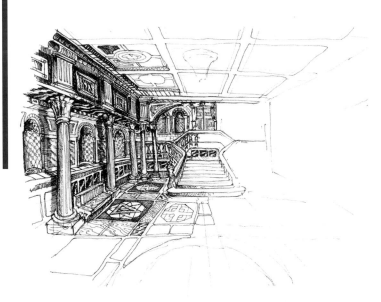

She's a Killer Queen

Gunpowder, gelatine

Dynamite with a laser beam

Guaranteed to blow your mind...

In conversation she spoke

just like a Baroness...

Drop of a hat she's as willing

as a playful pussy cat

Then momentarily out of action...

She's out to get you...

Killer Queen

THE BARONESS

The Baroness - a hideous octogenarian whose wrinkled face is pasted in white powder, whose greying hair is hidden by a grand wig and two tight black horns of hair, sore melted eyes reflect the corruption and dreadful mortality below her parchment skin. She is known and feared as the Killer Queen. She surrounds herself with bloated luxury, riches, jewels, and young lovers.

The corridor from the ballroom to the Baroness's boudoir.

THE BARONESS AND HER BOUDOIR

"Well done. I detect a certain....scent about you." So says the Baroness when Dubroc breathlessly bursts into her chamber. She disappears into the bathroom while Dubroc stands, contemplating his next move.

The boudoir matches the rampant opulence of the downstairs. Vast windows provide the main light source in the room, staining the marbled floors and the four-poster bed with emblems of distorted chivalry.

THE CRYSTAL PALACE

The twisted environs of the Crystal Palace are one of the main areas of the Works Domain.

It's magnificent exterior conceals a black heart. The Crystal Palace is a horror. The air is rank with the humidity of rotting plants. Condensation mats the windows. A mist clogs the air, floating over the greasy tiled floor, inscribed with Tarot symbols and Masonic effigies. A shock of overgrown plants sprawl over their gardens, their leaves clutching at the walkways and balconies. In the centre of this dead palace is the Power orb, a wrought iron obelisk. A huge gallery with steelwork frames arches off into the distance.

THE THEATRE DOMAIN

Once again, Dubroc finds himself in another world. These are the haunted environs of a deserted Victorian theatre. Here is a Queen Domain on the brink of being dissolved by the evil of Death On Two Legs. Already the cobwebs of corruption drift through the half-light. The echoes of past productions reverberate between footsteps. Ghosts and zombies prowl the aisles. Trap doors, dead ends, and blind corners distort the architecture. The Theatre Domain has become an emporium of evil.

The Theatre is deserted. Voices from the past spill through the walls - snatches of dialogue, melodrama, anguish - leak from the fibres of the building. Aged stage sets lie broken and discarded. Costumes rot on the floor. Old posters are peeling from the wall, leaving discoloured sores in the paintwork. The chair covers are dusty and threadbare.

Most of the structure remains intact, the layers which make up the theatre still interconnect. Beyond the foyer are the auditorium and the stalls, circled by the side boxes and balconies. Below the stage and the wings is the orchestra pit, behind which lie the dressing rooms. Secret passages and false floors give access to the hidden, blackened heart of the dying playhouse.

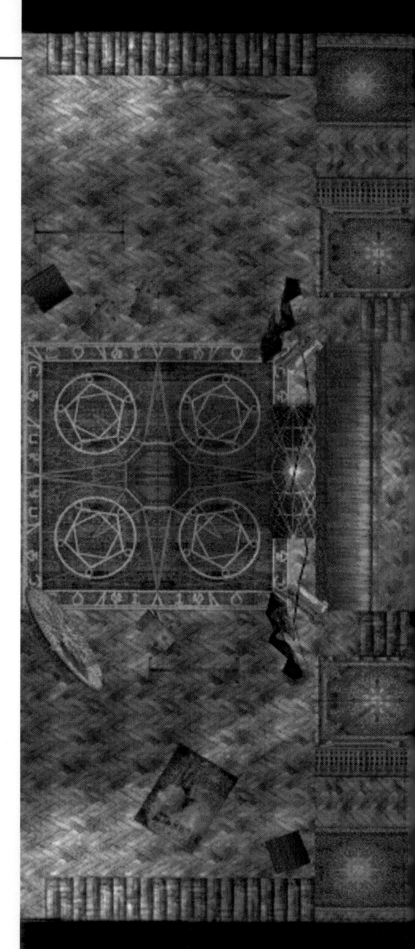

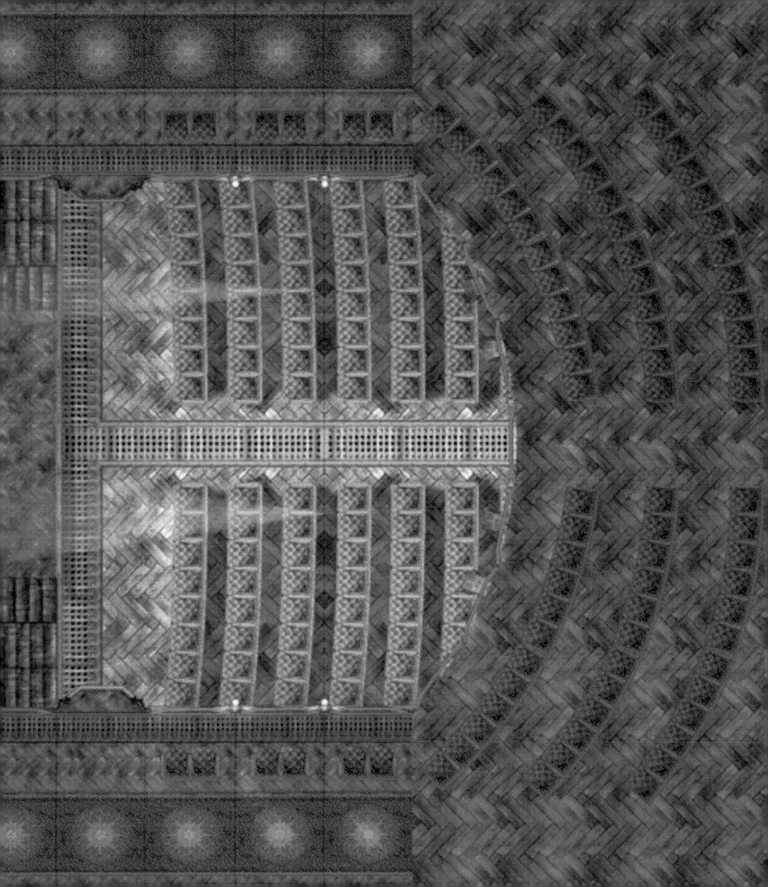

The traditional colour scheme of claret, ivory and gold still remains, bleeding through the furniture, carpets, and walls. Once a celebration of glory, passion, and entertainment, the colour scheme has become warped. The claret has thickened to blood-red, the ivory is stained yellow, and the gold has faded. Flickering oil lamps and carriage lights line the walls. The Art Deco ambience is deadened by the impoverished lighting. The Ticket Booth is empty and boarded up, a reminder of the theatre's once glorious past. Carvings bolster the foyer, lining the steps which lead to the upper levels and balconies.

There are four sets of doors. The main archway leads through to the auditorium. At the peak of the stairs are the doors to the royal boxes. One set is chained. Behind are the heavy-set entrance portals leading to the outside. They have been sealed.

Outlandish and overpowering, the auditorium throbs with Victorian architecture. A fleeting rain of light rays descend from the spotlights above. Vague black shadows coat the seating. The dress circle is masked in gloom. The huge circular stage is framed by a red luminous Proscenium Arch and backed with rich red velvet curtains. A central carpeted aisle cuts through the stalls, and leads to the orchestra pit. Dust flares in the spotlights. The smell of death and bones leadens the air.

The settings for the Theatre Zone was partly based on the antique Playhouse in Charing Cross, London, which was used for the *A Kind Of Magic* video. The architecture and dusty glory of this location was combined with the garish horror of the Hammer House movie, Theatre Of Blood, where Vincent Price plays a murderous actor who systematically murders all his critics. The whole scene was rounded off with touches and architectural nuances from a variety of classic theatres and performances, especially Artaud's Theatre Of Cruelty and the thick tradition of London East-End vaudeville.

The side boxes gives the best view of the mouldy auditorium, but are exposed and dangerous.

Behind the stage hangs a huge curtain. Painted on its surface is a spotlit image of Mestopholies' face, his eyes burning with malevolence. Dotted here and there are posters displaying grotesque characters and warped clownish faces. Costumes, props and stage lights clutter the spaces.

THE DRESSING ROOM

The dressing room areas are accessed from the wings and house the theatre paraphernalia. Each room is associated with a specialist act. Posters from these acts are glued to the walls.

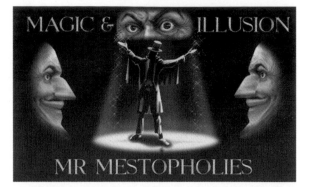

FLY FLOOR

A nested mass of scaffolding and platforms, the Fly Floor rises above the stage. Although sturdy and well made, age has weakened its supports. Too much disturbance and the entire thing may give way.

THE SAWN LADY
Lady Luck to her friends, The Sawn Lady is a traditional female assistant to Mestopholies, dressed in fine silk.

THE WINGS

Sandwiched between the voluminous stage curtains and the theatre walls are the wings. Lugubrious, dank, and mouldy, the wings are stained with the overspill of malevolence from the stage. A set of constatina doors marks one wall. Underused theatre lights and costume racks obstruct the other. The walls are slimy, the metal struts rusted. High above, the distressed suspended ceiling leans threateningly.

THE INNUENDO DOMAIN

Throughout the Queen domains, Dubroc has been exposed to a torrent of unchecked creativity. All through his adventure, he has been fought by strange creatures, and pushed to the limit by arcane puzzles and traps. Endlessly, he has interacted with the characters who inhabit the Domains and has been drawn inexorably into their wars and disputes.

Nothing, however, can prepare him for the sinister beauty of this Queen Domain. So long suppressed by the Eye and so long a toy of Death On Two Legs, the Innuendo Domain is a surreal tour-de-force, an hallucinogenic dream.

A sprawling Victorian circus, packed with stands and side-shows, circles a garish big top. There is an autumnal flavour in the cold air. The lights and glowing colours of the stands creep across the twilight. A tenuous mist floats above the ground. As Dubroc draws closer though, he can see the strange flatness of the buildings, the inanimate shadows behind the counters, and the disturbing, deadly quiet dampening the whole area.

The Fairground is made up of outlandish Victorian circus stalls. Like a Grandeville illustration, the ring of stands and kiosks glare out of the hazy, impenetrable fog. All the facades - Madame Magritte's Fortune Telling kiosk, the Cranium Crackers, The Hammer Test - are like flat canvases, cardboard cut-outs which only stir into life when something living passes by. Scaffolding can be seen behind some structures. Skeletal trees rear into the cloudy, overcast sky, stained red with some hideous frozen mixture of dawn and dusk.

THE BIG TOP

The huge marquee dominates the fairground - 'The Greatest Show On Earth'. Its magnificent fabrics glimmer in the wind. Flags and bunting circle its outside. Thick ropes hold it in place. Only darkness shows through its portal, but its size and sumptuousness hint at pleasures and excitement within.

THE MERRY GO ROUND
No fairground would be complete without the spinning fun of a Merry Go Round. Unfortunately nothing is normal in the Innuendo Domain.

MR ELECTRO
A giant robotic machine, Mr Electro is in dire need of a power supply. His huge, brightly coloured form stands silent and inert, waiting for that small spark which will set him free. He is an overgrown toy with kaleidoscope eyes and a square box for a mouth.

MADAME MAGRITTE

One of the only real people left in the Innuendo Domain is Madame Magritte, the resident Fortune Teller, confined by fear to her stall. She has heard the cries of pain and the giggling of the clowns in the mist. She sits at her table, before her a crystal ball and a tablet of alchemic symbols. A huge tarot card adorns one wall.

MADAM
MARGARITE

THE WHEEL OF FORTUNE
The Wheel stands alluringly in one corner of the circus.

THE CRANIUM CRACKERS
In the Innuendo Domain, nothing is normal. The Cranium Cracker (Coconut Shy), most simple and enjoyable of all fairground attractions, has been twisted and warped. The coconuts have been replaced by animated heads, which talk in chirpy cockney rhyming slang.

McGRUE'S HAMMER TEST
This stall is designed as a trial of strength - only the brave need apply. It is minded by Iron Man McGrue, a huge old-fashioned weight-lifter dressed in a Victorian swim suit. His huge torso looks gigantic as it towers over his tiny waist. His face is round and bulbous.

THE BEARDED COCKROACH
This esoteric stall is a play on the Guess-The-Weight challenges. A giant scarab sits on a pair of scales, inert and dormant, as if made of stone. Three objects lay before the scales.
A rasping mechanical voice speaks: "How much ? How much do I weigh?"

THE FINAL DOMAIN

Once dubroc has navigated his way through the other domains, he finds himself in the heart of the Network. This immense cavern bristles with technology, radiating pulses of energy. It is here that the Eye has manifested itself. It is here that the final conflict will take place.

Leading to the heart of the cavern is a mile long corridor. Energy bolts and warning devices line the floors and walls. The defence mechanism is akin to that of the human body, only this time it is Dubroc which is the alien infection.

Once inside the cavern Dubroc is confronted by a maze like structure. In the centre is the Eye. Now forewarned of his presence it will activate the final challenge which Dubroc must overcome.

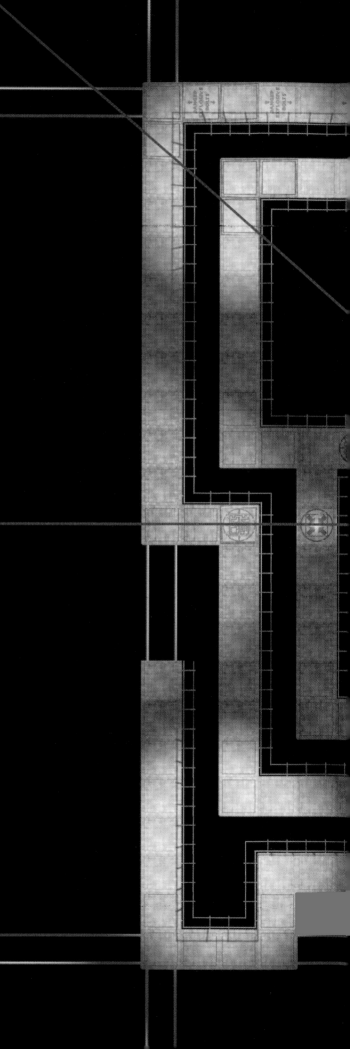

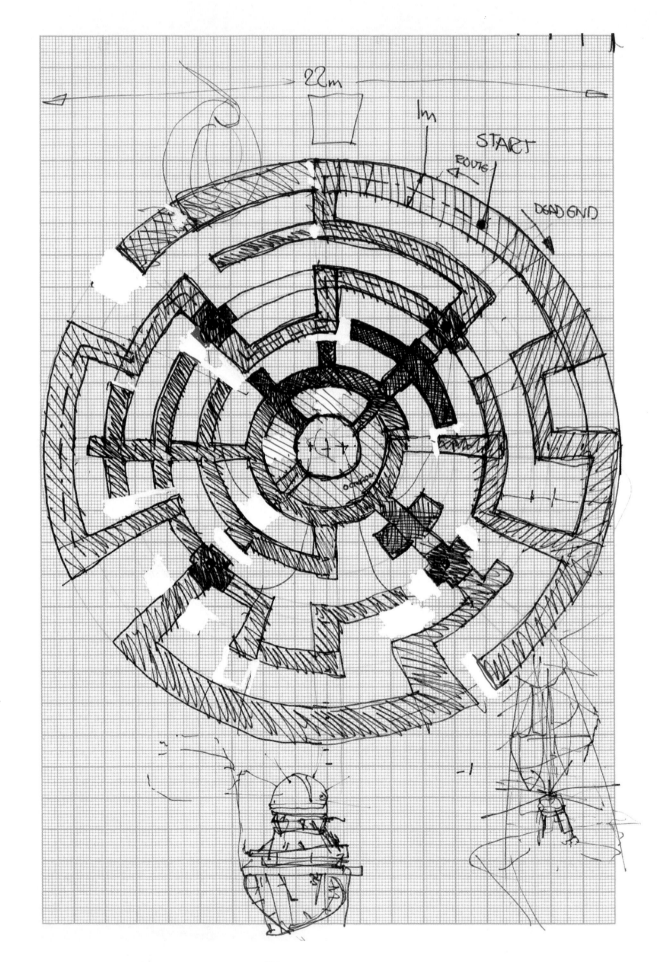

*Original floor plan
sketch of the cavern.*

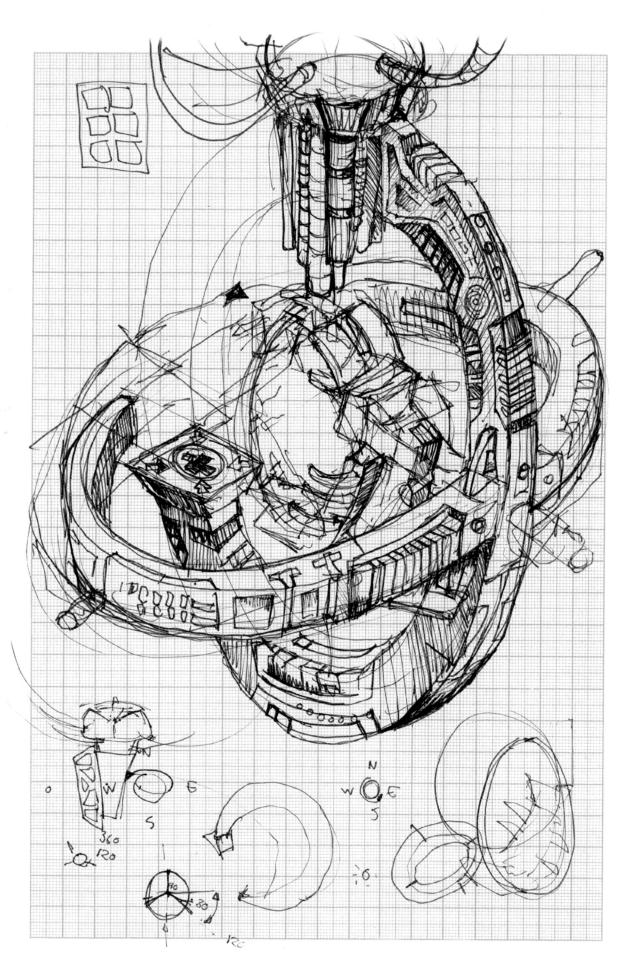

Concept sketch of the centre of the cavern.

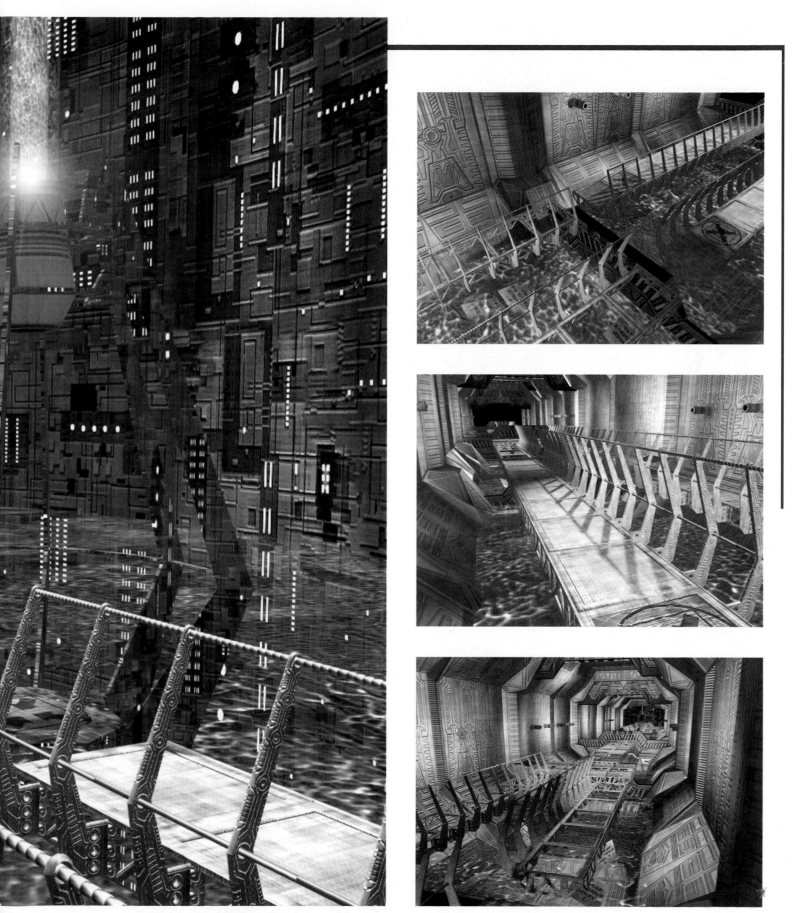

The end cages which descend into the heart of the cavern.

MOTION CAPTURE

Queen: The Eye is a game which straddles two distinct genres - the fighting game and the adventure game. The two blend seamlessly. The combat is as distinctive and realistic as the backdrops. The moves are dramatic, life-like. The characters express emotion as they animate. There's a certain grace to the body language. An unmistakable style to the action.

This level of artistry is only achievable one way. Every movement in the game, every step forward, every turned head, every raised arm, has been painstakingly recorded from the movements of a single real-life actor, using the latest cutting-edge technology - Motion Capture.

Characterisation and animation of the human form is the next stage for the gaming industry and the only way to achieve it convincingly is with motion capture. For the game, the team used the latest technology to allow them to reach an artistic middle-ground with the in-game graphics. They are striving for flamboyant yet solid movement, maintaining the style and character in Dubroc motions, alongside the drama and athleticism of combat, without losing realism or playability en route.

The whole system works around a single actor. He stands topless, dotted with tiny white balls. Thirty two in total - on his forehead, shoulders, chest, hands, feet, arms and legs. These are light-sensitive diodes, electronic boils seen only by the eight infra-red cameras which circle him. As the actor moves, each camera notes the changing position of the dots and relays pulses of information to a state-of-the-art workstation in the corner, where it is digitised and compiled into visual form. The panoramic layout of the cam-

eras allows the computer to work out the three-dimensional location of each dot, while their hi-resolution capabilities allow the capture of incredibly accurate and clean shapes and motion, used later to build a fully rounded moving 3D figure.

THE SHOOT

Like every artistic technique, Motion Capture is a torturous process. It takes skill and experience to direct, agility and stamina to enact, and incredible patience to perfect. Each move, no matter how slight or subtle, produces megabytes of information. Each burst of data is spooled onto the computer's hard-disk and stored for processing at a later date. Conversion into an useable animation will happen later. Right now, there is only time to get through the hundreds of actions the game demands.

A list of seven hundred and fifty moves has been drawn up, from very simple moves such as walking forward and turning, through to break-falls and weapon reloading. The actions have been split into two main categories. Basic moves cover jumping, punching and kicking as well as moving to and from the basic combat stance.

The second category contains more complicated work - the special moves which are the backbone of any combat game. Dubroc

develops as the story progresses. He gets stronger and faster. He's upgraded with better weapons and moves. His reaction to hits varies depending on how tough he is. All the minutiae of these individual shots have to be designed, scheduled, performed, and somehow fitted into a lunch-less five day schedule.

To act out both the fighting and more mundane moves, Destination Design avoided hiring the usual karate or kung fu based martial artist, and opted instead for William Timms, a 3rd Dan Aikido teacher. He fitted the bill because his martial abilities suited the philosophy behind the character of Dubroc.

Aikido perfectly suits the style of the game, embracing the players' motives and encounters. The ancient Japanese art is completely designed around self-defence, and opts for subtle movements, shifts in balance, and short sharp shocks to disable or maim opponents. Every single technique has an underlying self-defence aspect. Aikido is also the martial art of choice for the Japanese and UK police forces - and Dubroc is, technically, an ex-policeman.

The motion capture system enables the team to record the full dynamics of acrobatic movement.

Compared with other motion capture systems, the pioneering technology used by Destination Design works with amazingly small diodes. In other set-ups, the balls are typically eight times the size. The smaller dots gives the team a much greater fluidity of movement and a greater degree of flexibility. The actor also has more freedom of movement. There are no wires to restrain him, and his more acrobatic movements don't damage the tiny dots.

But, despite this flexibility, the shoot is hard graft. Over five long and sweaty days, William is directed through a host of different moves, sometimes with three or four takes per move. He's asked to make dramatic the most insignificant of actions. He has to perform stunts he'd never dream of doing. He break-falls down stairs. He lets off a round of machine gun fire. Even the kicks prove to be a challenge.

Motion capture is an abstract concept. It's essentially the process of recording the hidden grace of the body. Subtle movements, body language, and expressions are all captured digitally. It's easy to achieve the percussive combat moves - kicks, punches, elbow strikes. It's not the hyper-kinetic kicks and throws, nor the wielding of swords or machete throwing which flummox the performer. The more subtle, natural actions prove to be the main problem.

In one situation, William has to pick up an object. A problem arises. The object hasn't been defined yet, so they're using a pretend object, a juggling ball. William has to imagine he's found the object on a table. Naturally, the animation doesn't look quite right. Paradoxically, he has to mime in a non-exaggerated way. William's body's not sure what it's doing. His limbs hesitate. His body halts. Also, to complicate matters further, the moves often have to be performed with emotion. William is asked to pick up objects furtively, or to convey that he is being hunted or chased. A substantial amount of mime and drama goes into each move.

POST-PRODUCTION
After a ten-hours-a-day week of shadow boxing, falling down stairs, being shot, collapsing, getting up again, jumping abysses, and looking furtive, hunted, and chased while pummelling an imaginary gladiator to the ground, the shoot is complete. The swathes of motion capture data - over 500 megabytes - are parceled up and sent to Dijon, France where a team of specialists in human movement and software engineering, work for weeks to convert the mass of moving pixels into recognisable forms, using the cutting-edge Elite System of motion capture.

For simple movements - a raised arm, a turn of the head - the decoding process is quick and easy, usually taking around ten minutes. For a complex throwing manoeuvre or a break-fall, which can produce entire constellations of data, it takes hours or even days to manicure into shape. Using videos shot alongside the motion capture as a visual reference, the scientists painstakingly match up each dot to the joints on the actor's body. Frame-by-frame, they achingly form a wireframe stickman out of the chaos.

Five months down the line, when the motion capture data arrives in huge megabyte mouthfuls at Destination Design HQ, the animator builds a 3D representation using photographs and measurements taken at the shoot. For the animation to work, each dot on the 3D mesh has to correspond exactly to the dots on his body. It has to be millimetre-perfect. Luckily the team are aided by the nature of the martial art itself. All the energy and movement of Aikido comes from the hip area. This fits perfectly with their 3D model, where the pelvis area forms of the root of the hierarchical link, and the pivot point which originates all the movement.

Most of the unbelievable moves in popular arcade beat'em ups have not really been performed by motion-captured stunt men. The moves have been heavily tweaked and exaggerated in post-production. For Queen: The Eye, the artists spend weeks testing, correcting, and re-testing the animations by hand, ensuring that the joints move correctly, that the characters don't 'moonwalk', and - above all - that the sequences look convincing and dramatic. And furtive. And confident. And happy.

THE PROCESS
The first move to be worked on is a straight walking animation to check whether the character is working from an aesthetic point of view.

Luckily it's all in a day's work for an Aikido teacher. William actually likes falling. He's been doing it since he was a child, and it has become second nature to him. This is proved when, in the end, the move proves to be a one-take walkover. William launches himself from half-way up the steps, rolls down the length of a mat, and comes to a standing position at the bottom.

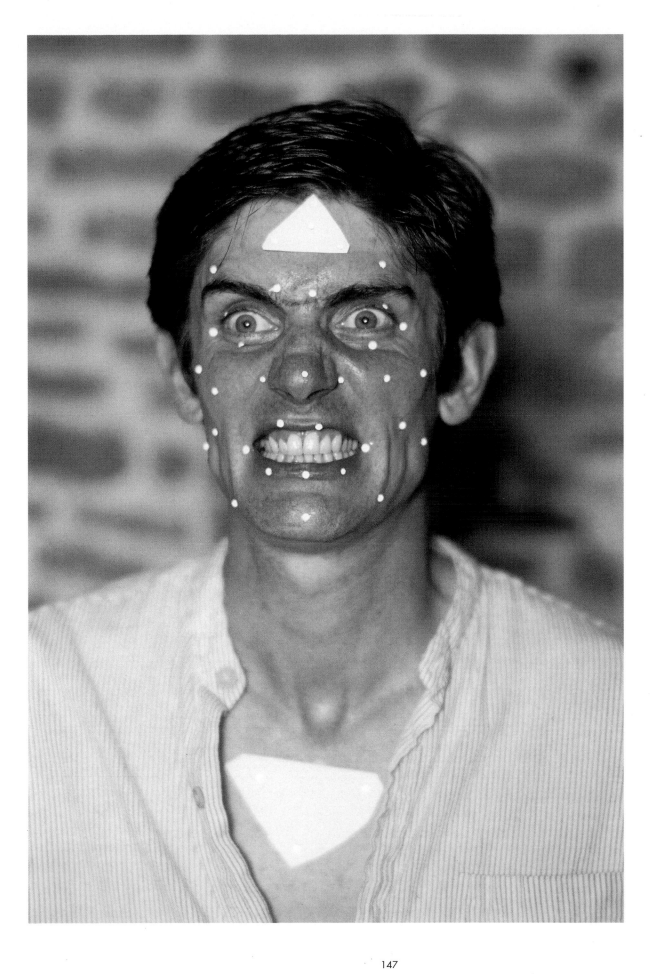

Motion capture was also used for full facial animation. This had never been done before.

WEAPONS & COMBAT

Adventure seeker on an empty street
Just an alley creeper, light on his feet
A young fighter screaming, with no time for doubt

I Want It All

ETHOS OF COMBAT

Queen: The Eye is an action adventure game. For every puzzle solved and every riddle deciphered, there is a long drawn-out battle to be fought. The motion captured fighting moves obviously draw a comparison with coin-op classics, but Queen: The Eye goes beyond these, providing for the first time, truly 'context-sensitive' combat. Dubroc fights only when he has to - when provoked or when a blatantly aggressive foe is blocking his way to an object. And he fights in keeping with the narrative, fights to fulfil a purpose, for a true reward, and, above all, fights in character.

The combat in Queen:The Eye looks every bit as stunning as its console counterparts, and is easily as much fun for those who want fast action shots of adrenaline. But for those looking for more, the game provides a much greater atmosphere. Throughout the Queen Domains, Dubroc is relentlessly stalked either by Death On Two Legs or by an army of roaming incidental characters, itching to burst into violence. The sense of urgency in the Arena is palpable. Dubroc is being hunted down. He has the option to run, the option to hide, the option to find a weapon, or the option to stand and fight. And when he does, he has a massive range of Aikido-based attacks and classic special moves to draw on.

Unlike most beat'em up protagonists, Dubroc does not simply support an excessive range of kicks and punches. Instead, he uses basic atemi or percussive strikes to vital areas to disable and maim his foes, using his knuckles, the heel of his hand, the palm, the elbow, and the knee - or deadly combinations of them all. Then, when he finds a weapon such as a sword, or a spear, he learns more moves - bokken moves with the blade, and effective attacks with clubs and machetes. Some weapons work better against certain opponents, but it's up to Dubroc to learn which ones. While Dubroc is as comfortable with a handgun or a crossbow as he is with his closed fist or knee, his most effective moves are throws, arguably the root of Aikido. These are the most difficult of all the attacks to achieve - requiring multiple key combinations - but by far the most impressive.

Above all, the main ethos running through the combat in Queen:The Eye is ensuring the violence is non-gratuitous. There's no blood or guts, broken limbs, or gore of any kind. In modern games as in B-movies, excessive gore just looks tacky and cheap.

WEAPON DESIGN

The concept behind the weapons in Queen: The Eye is simple: you can forearm yourself with a weapon before a battle but if you get hit, you lose it. There's greater skill in unarmed combat, but the game offers you the freedom to use a gun should you desire.

The gun design took some thought. Often, in the game, when Dubroc is on the periphery of a camera view, his weapon can be little more than a few pixels in size. Both in close-up and in far-view, the guns had to look weighty, meaty. They had to look as if Dubroc was carrying a weapon or something aggressive in his hand. Also, in fitting with the bleak industrialised canopy of the Arena, the design of futuristic hardware had to tread a thin line between the squeaky Buck Roger's look and the grimy handguns of Blade Runner and other sci-fi movies. The art team finally settled on a semi-industrial look with a steel plated design and with an old-fashioned, almost Victorian finish.

Most of the guns have been designed with simple functionality in mind - pistols, rifles, machine guns, and so on - but the artists allowed their imagination to run riot with a few choice piece of military hardware. They also played with the idea of resurrecting the old fashioned railgun, one of the first semi-automatic weapons, which used a linear accelerator to fire out a red-hot ingot of metal. That was dropped.

The majority of the weapons in the game, however, remain the classic physical devices, which required skill and martial art to wield effectively - the sword, the machete, the crossbow, the crowbar, and the club.

THE OPPONENTS

Wherever Dubroc goes within the Queen Domains he is guaranteed a fight. In the Arena it is the Watchers and the guards who form a long queue to take Dubroc out. In the Works Domain, the thugs and the Lover Prince take over. In the Theatre Domain, the ghouls are Dubroc's main combatants, while in the surreal Innuendo Domain, the terrifying clowns are out to get him. Ultimately, in the Final Domain, he has the final manifestation of Death On Two Legs to face.

Most of the individual opponents have their own sets of moves, plucked from the hundred stored during the mammoth motion-capture shoot, mixed with standard kicks and punches. The Watchers have special moves to deal with their unique weaponry, while the clowns and the thugs share a similar monstrously hulking gait. The Zombies and Theatre Ghosts fight in that mindlessly lurching way the undead do, and the various guardians of special objects around the domains - SnakeMan and the Lover Prince for example - have their own idiosyncratic attacks.

Each character is endowed with a level of artificial intelligence (A.I.). Some of Dubroc's antagonists roam and patrols mindlessly. They are easy to kill. Some don't roam, protect a certain area, and carry weapons. These are harder to kill. Some move faster than others. Some have a wider range of possible moves and will react accordingly to Dubroc's attacks. Some have dialogue and responses - some don't. Effective A.I. is difficult to achieve with today's home computers, so the programmers of Queen: The Eye have used a simple trick to circumvent the problem and add a certain realism to the characters movement and combat reactions. They record themselves moving and attacking with the character, and then combine those patterns of movement with some custom A.I. routines. The result: some disturbingly unpredictable opponents who will anticipate and out-manoeuvre a complacent Dubroc.

REAL TIME OBJECTS

Before the weapons are discovered by Dubroc, they exist as 'real-time objects'. These are shapes and objects, as opposed to the painted backdrops, that the characters can interact with. Push around, pick up, or - in the case of the real-time blades - duck to avoid. Despite their relatively small size (most of the meshes are about one thousandth the size of the Arena model), each real-time object has been painstakingly conceived, built, and then textured for maximum realism. The restrictions on the size and shape are very strict. No object can have more than 100 faces, while most are forced down to around 50-60 faces to speed the game up.

The texture maps used have to be very small, as they have to be stored on the game CDs where space is at a premium. And finally, they will have to rotate and move within the game and keep their geometric accuracy as the camera angles change.

The muzzle flash in the game was simply created by painting a bright 2-D onto a 3D object shaped like a gunshot flare. Flicked into existence very briefly with the appropriate deafening sound effect creates an incredibly convincing illusion of real gun fire.

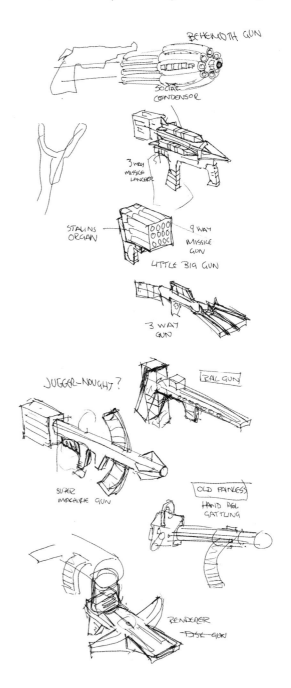

THE ART OF 3D

It looks stunning. It looks realistic. The floors glisten with light. The ceilings rear up into darkness. Objects throw long macabre shadows across the pock-marked walls. The sun peeps through a fog-encrusted window. The metal looks tortured, worn. A layer of mist floats above the granite paving stones. Water shimmers. The threat of danger hangs in the air. The scene is serene, beautiful - a mask for brutal dangers beyond.

It's not easy to express menace through architecture, or drama with shadows, or danger through lighting without being cliched. Using the latest 3D technology and modelling techniques, and guided by producer Richard Ashdown, Rapid Eye Movement Limited - the artists behind the art of Queen: The Eye - have striven for months to reach this delicate balance between palpable beauty and intangible danger. In the game, Dubroc finds himself in an alternate reality, a chaotic mix of archaic architecture, futuristic technology, and subconscious symbols. The worlds have to be realistic enough to grab the player, but simultaneously obtuse and out-of-sync enough to convey the rich heritage of imagery which surrounds Queen's music.

These images have been created using the latest technology and thousands of pounds worth of hardware, but it's a common misconception that technology is displacing the skill and talent from art, that anyone can pick up a computer a create photo-realistic 3D vistas with a few clicks of the mouse. The truth is that 3D images, with the quality and artistic sensibilities of those in Queen: The Eye, take months to conceive and huge amounts of talent and experience to realise.

THE TOOLS OF THE TRADE

While the 3D art and effects of many games and films are constructed with incandescently expensive Silicon Graphics workstation with programs like SoftImage and WaveFront, Rapid Eye Movement Limited predominately use Autodesk 3D Studio, the flagship of PC rendering, an immensely powerful but simple package which runs on most home PCs.

3DS is used like a film studio. In one part of the studio, in the modeller or 'workshop', the objects and the sets are constructed. Then using painting packages - such as Adobe PhotoShop - alongside another module within 3D Studio, the objects are given materials or 'texture-mapped' with realistic surfaces - such as wood, rocks, plastic etc. Eventually, after much refining, the objects are placed within a virtual 'stage', and cameras and lights positioned, finely tuned to illuminate and shape the set, just like a scene from a movie or a still photograph.

Overall though, as in any artistic pursuit, the actual program or the tools you use are not as important as the talent and imagination of the person behind the wheel. As long as the artist can picture the object, effect, or building in their head, and convert that to three dimensions on screen, then it is achievable; no matter how gratuitous or esoteric it may be.

It may sound like a simple process, but it's not. Aspects such as effective lighting or frame composition are disciplines which take time and practice to nurture, and each separate task - modelling, texture-mapping, framing, and rendering - is a skill in itself.

MODELLING

A couple of the main modellers on the project have architectural degrees, garnered after five years hard work at university, followed by two years work experience. The two had made the unusual side-step from commercial building design to virtual reality worlds after becoming disillusioned with the non-creativity of standard architecture. 3D game modelling had given them the chance to build thing's they'd always dreamed of and could never in the real world - a crystal palace, a Renaissance ballroom, a Gothic tower, a Victorian circus. All with the added bonus of avoiding builders, fire regulations, and skirting boards.

Their 'real-life' training has given them a massive advantage in this field. They have absorbed and studied square miles of architecture, and have been trained to look at the geometry and shape of objects, and to appreciate the underlying logic and simplicity of most structures. They are the perfect 3D modellers

In modelling, the 3D wireframe objects - or meshes - are built from two main components - primitives or splines. Primitives are simple geometric shapes which form the root of most forms in the real world. They are the sphere, the cone, the cylinder, the cube, and the torus (doughnut). Using these, either by intersecting or subtracting one shape from another, you can build almost any object you require - be it astrolabe, ground vehicle, spear, guitar, or an entire building with furniture.

If the objects avoid the basic forms, is made up of curves, or simply needs to look more organic, then things become more complicated. Objects like kettles or girders or anything man made which follows simple rules of geometry and straight-lines are effortless to build. The challenges come in modelling realistic and natural-looking organic objects. In this case, modellers have to rely on 'splines'.

Splines are curves used to draw a cross section of an object. The form is fine-tuned by tugging on anchor points dotted around the contours of the shape. Then the flat shape is extruded - or lofted - into three dimensions. 3D Studio has a set of 'deluxe extrusions' which have come in very handy for creating some of the bizarre objects in the game. Cross-sections are often drawn to a tip or sculptured with 'lathe' tool around a virtual potter's wheel. The possibilities are endless.

When the artists are stuck with 'modeller's block', they usually turn to the real-world for inspiration. As a result, the game is peppered with 3D objects and buildings which were once based on real-life architecture. The Professor's Gaudi Tower is based on the Sacra Familia in Barcelona. The Islamic feel for the library in the Works Domain is drawn from real-life Moroccan mosques. The entire auditorium in the Theatre Domain is influenced by the now derelict PlayHouse in Charing Cross in London (as used in the *A Kind Of Magic* video).

However, it's not a case of blatantly copying concepts. The modeller will often start off with a vague idea of how he wants the object to look, inspired from the brief given to him by the game's producer. He will bring in any effective shapes and clever touches he may have observed on buildings or in books, and with a rough visualisation in his head, he'll model an approximation of its shape, and then just tinker. Or leave it to stew. Often, the object develops so much over time that it ends up looking radically different from the first draft, changing like lines of dialogue might in the game.

TEXTURE MAPPING

The next step in any model's construction is applying surfaces. Textures - which can either be scans of photographs or computer-generated images - are what gives a model its realism. The attention paid to experimenting and finding the perfect surface can be the difference between a good or a bad model.

At the simplest level, objects are given a colour, and then endowed reflective qualities and shading. Many objects in the game - such as plastic railings, chairs, or plain walls - don't need texture maps as they meant to look flat and unremarkable. Other objects, however, demand layers of special mapping techniques. The surface of each element in a scene can be made luminous so that it radiates light, or shiny so that it catches and reflects the illumination around it. For a more organic feel, a texture can be roughed up, scattering light across its surface, or be given specular highlights such as those found on naturally reflective surfaces like water and

glass. For a realistic touch, objects such as lamps or windows can be made transparent.

Due to the rich tapestry of images and ornamental feel to the art of the game texture-maps were predominantly used on the 3D objects. A mammoth library of materials was built up to use in the game, assembled from photographs taken from the countryside. Close-up shots of crates, gravel, metal, wood were scanned in, reworked, and used as a basic image resource in the final scenes. However, if the team needed a highly specific image - such as rotting white metal or symbols - one of the in-house artists drew or painted it from scratch, straight onto computer via a special tablet.

LIGHTING & CAMERA ANGLES

Once the location sets have been built and arranged with all the necessary objects and artwork, the scene is ready for the next stage - the placing of lights and cameras. Lighting is essential for giving a scene depth and realism and, as with every stage of the 3D design process, it can kill or revitalise a piece of work. Overlighting creates a white-wash; underlighting destroys the subtleties. Shadows too are integral to the feel of a scene. Harsh, sharp edged shadows create drama and menace. Softer more blurred shadows give a more relaxed, picturesque feel to the scene, enhancing the mood. The overall lighting is also important for maintaining the depth of field in a camera view. If you want to give a cavernous or a claustrophobic air to the scenery, you have to light it properly.

There are three main types of lighting in the game. Ambient light is the general illumination which saturates the scene. The artists use its intensity (from daylight to dusk) to 'fill' out scenic details, and, in areas like the sewers and prison cells, it is down-played to give a menacing contrast between the background and other lights in the scene. Bright scenes - such as the Crystal Palace or the Innuendo Domain - use spot lights to simulate sunlight or to create the patterned shadows of stained glass windows as in the Baroness' Boudoir. Omni lights are placed inside bulbs or near to torches to emulate the effects of a unshielded bulb, radiating light in all directions, and creating minor atmospheric touches. Lens flares are added in post production to give more depth and realism, especially in the Ballroom and the Arena.

Spotlights are the most powerful of all the lights used in the game. providing focused beams of light, and allowing the artists to draw attention to certain areas of a scene. These are used to great effect in the Arena, creating circles of dangers and areas of vulnerability which Dubroc must avoid, and illuminating the stark deadliness of the architecture.

To finish off each scene, the team set up a variety of camera positions. The views from these lens will be used in the finished game. Cameras with various types of lenses and fields of view can be created. Each domain uses over one hundred different angles, framed for their splendour, for their drama, or to maintain continuity as Dubroc wanders around the rendered universe.

RENDERING

The last stage in the process is rendering. This is the point where the artists finally see the fruits of their labour in all its glory. Computer RAM memory and processing speed are the currencies here. The camera views are rendered on Pentium PCs, each with 128 megabytes of RAM - but even with this high-end set-up the rendering times are unpredictable. Any number of factors can bloat the times, but the simple rule is - the larger and more realistic the scene, the longer it takes to render. This can mean waiting times from two to forty-five minutes for each camera angle, depending on the number of lights, image maps, and shadows which have to be calculated. During rendering the workstation's processor goes into overdrive, scanning through the scene and computing how each face of each object will react to the lighting and how it should reflect its surroundings. It shrinks and twists the texture-maps to fit, works out the penumbras of the shadows, and finally 'anti-aliases' the entire picture, minutely smoothing out all the models' jagged edges.

Three-quarters of an hour may not sound that long for a final image, but when you consider that there are over five hundred views in the game, you can see that the machines could take over two weeks to process the required scenes.

The number of faces in a scene are kept as low as possible, and a variety of low resolution previews are performed to check that each angle looks good, and that the shadows and lights are working. The previews are generally 'gouraud shaded' - which is a quick way of seeing how lights and objects mix in a scene. It uses different shades of the same colour to approximate light and dark areas in the image. For the final game graphics however the team use 'metal' shaded scenes which provide the ultimate in realism.

One of the most ground-breaking features of Queen: The Eye is the incredible merging of technology with classic story-telling. A classical tale of triumph over adversity, exploration and discovery, and vengeance has been told with images and sound of a quality never before seen in video game entertainment. One of the major achievements of the development team has been the incorporation of true characters into the 3D world. Not just motion-captured mannequins or a series of body parts jammed together in different combinations. The forty personalities which inhabitant the Queen Domains have their own idiosyncrasies, their own expressions, their own voices, and their own physical appearances. They are clearly distinguishable from each other and move about with motive and purpose. They are characters.

SKETCHES

Each character has been outlined in the script for the game and, taking them one by one, the artists look to various sources for inspiration - people they know, television, films and comics, the Queen videos and, of course, their own imagination. Occasionally for the simple characters such as Cosimo The Thug or the Snake Man, the idea comes straight away and develops little from paper to pixel, but usually, the character goes through several changes before it's ready to be converted into 3D.

At an early stage, a cartoonist is drafted in to explore the characters in the game - how best their personalities could be expressed by their physical appearance and clothing. The resulting sketches are obviously too avant-garde and stylised to be rendered into 3D, so the artists use them as a basis for their own drawings, and 'tone' them down so they can be rebuilt on the virtual stage.

A good example of this process is Cosimo the Thug from the Works Domain who began life as a stout, cartoonish thug with a pirate-esque look. A huge scar descends down one side of his face, neatly intersecting the mottled sea of stubble on his thick jaw. He wears a Skull & Crossbones jerkin, a waistcoat, and a dagger. His biceps and forearms are huge and his face is crumpled with unintelligent, thuggish glee.

The artists take this comically expressive sketch and develop Cosimo into a crisper, more realistic figure, retaining the main features of the original - the jaw, the biceps, the slumping gait - and merely translating essence of the character and menace of the first sketch into a easier form to render on computer.

And then finally the model is built and coloured.

BUILDING THE HEADS

The face of course says the most about a person, so the next character-building step is to form the head and faces of the games' denizens. The personalities are still developing and, as the environments too start to emerge, the two begin to feed off each other. One of the artists, who may be working on the architectural highlights of one domain, may see the way a character is changing, and adapt the scenery to suit the colours, or tones, or impression of the character. For instance, the sketches of Mestopholies were finished before the Theatre Domain was designed. So the auditorium, the crypt and the other elements of that domain were built around him, reflecting his warped mind and fastidious showmanship.

A default head was built in three dimensions in 3D Studio. Although it was a relatively simple model - made up of only 250 faces - it took two weeks to build because it had to as versatile as a lump of clay so that it could be pushed and pulled into over forty radically-different facial forms.

Points placed on key locations such as the nose, forehead, cheeks, eyes and chin allowed the artists to sculpt the wireframes of the model into almost any form, from the wizened hooked face of the Fakir to the bloated masks of Monsieur Mongolfier.

Finally, the textures were prepared, ready to be mapped onto the finished face model. Some faces were hand painted. Some were created on computer. Some were both. All were wrapped around the mesh, creating a staggeringly broad range of looks and characters.

DESTINATION 1995
design

RAVENS

IRON OWL

NERVOUS SAUSAGE DOG

SINGING FROG

BRASS SNAKE

STRANGE FLY CATCHING INSECT

CAT WITH DIAMOND NECKLACE

BRASS CLOCKWORK KILLER FROG

STREET RAT

BAT

Early concept sketches of characters which did not make the final game.

THE MUSIC

The iconography of Queen - their music, videos and art - have had a subtle yet profound effect on the look and feel of Queen: The Eye. Scattered throughout the game are little artistic touches - objects, icons, patterns - influenced by the videos and album covers produced over the years. More tangible, of course, are the characters inspired by the songs - Mr Fahrenheit, The Baroness, Death On Two Legs - accentuating gameplay already packed with clips and sequences soaked up from Queen promo films, plus the Domains and sections melding Queen albums with classic literature and architecture.

Working on the audio at Cosford Mill Studio.

But undoubtedly the main influence of Queen in the game is the soundtrack. Using re-mixes of well-known tracks alongside looped sections of more obscure titles and instrumentals, the game's music quite frankly goes beyond the music of any game in the last decade. Sometimes rousing, sometimes unnerving, sometimes fantastically emotive, the musical score lifts the game to new heights and brings the stunning visuals and characters to breath-taking life.

Over a month, the Queen archives were trawled to produce the songs and sound textures for the game.

The team uncovered a mass of suitable material from the incredibly sound-track friendly early albums, recorded before Queen embraced the synthesizer in *The Game*. The hard, driven rock and roll of the early days fitted perfectly with alternating rhythms of the gameplay, hard then soft, combat then puzzles. In particular, they tapped a rich vein of powerful themes and emotive sections on the *Jazz* album.

Strangely, the music does not hit you in the face as Queen. With the lyrics sometimes removed and the context often radically changed, the music itself changes, side-stepping from classic rock into exciting game soundtrack. Even the most hardened Queen aficionado will find it hard to recognise where some sequences have been pulled from.

THE ARENA
Before Dubroc can mix with the vibrant imagery of the Queen Domains, he must first navigate the Arena - the Domain least influenced visually by Queen, but featuring a vast sweep of music. In the game, music exhibits itself in two forms. Either as a straight background theme to bolster or shape the emotion or atmosphere of a scene, or as an unleashed burst of sound when Dubroc frees a musical archive. Both of these are used to great effect in the Arena. The main through-line for choosing the music for the Arena was to avoid songs which would have seemed obvious choices. So, as Dubroc is led through the entrance and into the first camera views, *I Want It All* sounds out, loud and defiant. Then as he picks his way from fight to fight, from mortal danger to fatal peril, a combination of themes assist him.

TRACK LISTING
More Of That Jazz (Taylor) – *Jazz*
In The Lap Of The Gods (Mercury) – *Sheer Heart Attack*
Modern Times Rock 'n' Roll (Taylor) – *Queen*
Fight From The Inside (Taylor) – *News Of The World*
Dragon Attack (May) – *The Game*
Party (Queen) – *The Miracle*
I Want It All (Queen) – *The Miracle*
Hang On In There (Queen) – *The Miracle*
Chinese Torture (Queen) – *The Miracle*
Liar (Mercury) – *Queen*
The Night Comes Down (May) – *Queen*

THE WORKS DOMAIN

The influence of Queen can be found all the way through the Works Domain. From the title right through to the plot of rebellion and resistance through radio, song references and images can be found everywhere. The clock in the museum is based on the one used in the *Radio Ga-Ga* Video. The Baroness is partly inspired by the song *Killer Queen*. The video prizes in this domain are *It's A Hard Life* and *Radio Ga-Ga* itself. Naturally, most of the key songs are taken from *The Works* album, topped with a championing chorus of *One Vision* to signal the successful completion of the level.

THE THEATRE DOMAIN

Perhaps the domain most blatantly drawn from Queen images is the Theatre Domain. The *A Kind Of Magic* video forms the unmistakable inspiration for the settings. The dank, defunct ancient theatre is a perfect chassis to portray the paranormal machinations of Death On Two Legs as Mr Mestopholies, while his alter-ego Leroy Brown - himself taken from the Queen track *Bring Back That Leroy Brown* - is portrayed during the game as being trapped in a mirror, using clips of Freddie Mercury in top hat and tails from the *A Kind of Magic* video. Images of the cherub and the skull were also taken from the video. The visual spectacle and over-the-top characters were perfectly in keeping with the theme of the domain.

TRACK LISTING

Tear It Up (May) – *The Works*
Machines (Or Back To Humans) (Taylor, May) – *The Works*
Hammer To Fall (May) – *The Works*
Keep Passing The Open Window (Mercury) – *The Works*
Tie Your Mother Down (May) – *A Day At The Races*
You Take My Breath Away (Mercury) – *A Day At The Races*
The Prophet's Song (May) – *A Night At The Opera*
Sweet Lady (May) – *A Night At The Opera*
It's Late (May) – *News Of The World*
Killer Queen (Mercury) – *Sheer Heart Attack*
One Vision (Queen) – *A Kind Of Magic*
Mother Love (May, Mercury) – *Made In Heaven*
Made In Heaven (Mercury) – *Made In Heaven*
Procession (May) – *Queen II*
Mustapha (Mercury) – *Jazz*
Was It All Worth It (Queen) – *The Miracle*

TRACK LISTING

Who Wants To Live Forever (May) – *A Kind Of Magic*
A Kind Of Magic (Taylor) – *A Kind Of Magic*
The Invisible Man (Queen) – *The Miracle*
Dreamers Ball (May) – *Jazz*
Gimme The Prize (Kurgans Theme) (May) – *A Kind Of Magic*
Don't Lose Your Head (Taylor) – *A Kind Of Magic*
Princes Of The Universe (Mercury) – *A Kind Of Magic*
Let Me Entertain You (Mercury) – *Jazz*
Bring Back That Leroy Brown (Mercury) – *Sheer Heart Attack*
Was It All Worth It (Queen) – *The Miracle*

THE INNUENDO DOMAIN

The torrent of hyper-surreal images and constructions found in the Innuendo Domain are inspired by the unique look and feel of the images which decorate *Innuendo* album. They themselves are drawn in homage of the Grandville illustrations of the 19th century. The cannon in the cornfield can be found on the back of the album cover while the Juggler is, of course, the key focus for the whole domain's imagery.

THE FINAL DOMAIN

A sense of pace and the gradual acceleration towards an apocalyptic climax were needed in this domain. *Breakthru* is the main theme here, echoing down the twisting corridors as Dubroc chases Death On Two Legs through the Network.

TRACK LISTING

Keep Passing The Open Windows (Mercury) – *The Works*
Brighton Rock (May) – *Sheer Heart Attack*
Innuendo (Queen) – *Innuendo*
You Don't Fool Me (Queen) – *Made In Heaven*
I Can't live With You (Queen) – *Innuendo*
The Hitman (Queen) – *Innuendo*
Khashoggi's Ship (Queen) – *The Miracle*
Heaven For Everyone (Taylor) – *Made In Heaven*
I'm Going Slightly Mad (Queen) – *Innuendo*
Bijou (Queen) – *Innuendo*
The Show Must Go On (Queen) – *Innuendo*
Too Much Love Will Kill You (May, Musker, Lamers) – *Made In Heaven*
Made In Heaven (Mercury) – *Made In Heaven*
Track 13 (Queen) – *Made In Heaven*
It's A Beautiful Day (Queen) – *Made In Heaven*

TRACK LISTING

Headlong (Queen) – *Innuendo*
Ride The Wild Wind (Queen) – *Innuendo*
Get Down Make Love (Mercury) – *News Of The World*
We Will rock You (May) – *News Of The World*
Bohemian Rhapsody (Mercury) – *A Night At The Opera*
Mother Love (May, Mercury) – *Made In Heaven*
Breakthru (Queen) – *The Miracle*
Death On Two Legs (Dedicated To...) (Mercury) – *A Night At The Opera*
Dancer (May) – *Hot Space*
Action This day (Taylor) – *Hot Space*
Las Palabras De Amor (The Words Of Love) (May) – *Hot Space*
Under Pressure (Queen, Bowie) – *Hot Space*
Put Out The Fire (May) – *Hot Space*
White Man (May) – *A Day At The Races*

 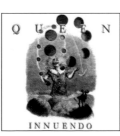